Curtain Call

A Comedy

Bettine Manktelow

A SAMUEL FRENCH ACTING EDITION

SAMUEL FRENCH

FOUNDED 1830

SAMUELFRENCH-LONDON.CO.UK
SAMUELFRENCH.COM

FOR AMATEUR PRODUCTION ENQUIRIES

UNITED KINGDOM AND WORLD EXCLUDING NORTH AMERICA

plays@SamuelFrench-London.co.uk

020 7255 4302/01

Each title is subject to availability from Samuel French,

depending upon country of performance.

CURTAIN CALL

First presented under the title *Stage Struck* by the Guild Players at the Kilshawe Theatre, Deal, Kent, on 15th July 1999, with the following cast:

Val Marshall	Coralie Kavanagh
Alec Partridge	Pip Piacentino
Lulu Lynchpin	Leita Cobb
Doreta Mason	Gilly Litton
Murphy	Tony Johnson
Rita	Louisa Jackson
Ms Murdstone	Christine Eyden
Clarence Mason	Peter Ryder

Directed by Bettine Walters

CHARACTERS

Valerie. The General Manager's secretary. She is thirtyish, attractive but with a distracted expression and a mournful air, pressure of work and her personal problems weighing on her mind. She is inclined to be tart and waspish but this is only because she is a lady with a problem as we discover during the course of the play.

Alec Partridge. The General Manager. He is about fifty, an affable, agreeable person, trying hard to keep up an appearance of imperturbability as he grapples with the seemingly insurmountable problems facing him with the day to day management of a provincial theatre. He tries to make light of all his problems by being bright and breezy at all times.

Lulu Lynchpin. The Stage Manager. She can be anything between thirty and fifty and is tough, wiry, capable, unflappable and dependable, the backbone of the theatre. When the play begins, however, she wears a worried air.

Doreta Mason. An ex-professional actress, glamorous, past her best but still trying hard. Initially she appears to be pretentious and superior, imperious and brittle, but underneath she is extremely vulnerable, as we discover during the play.

Murphy. The Front of House Manager, thirty-five. He is attractive, a flirt with an eye for the ladies, charming and sympathetic but not very energetic.

Rita. A barmaid and usherette. She is aged between twenty-five and thirty and has been through the mill. She is fussy, pretty, kind and just a little bit common, good-natured and popular with everybody.

Ms Murdstone. From the Arts Council. Any age. She is rather prim and severe, very conscious of her power and position.

Clarence Mason. A local councillor and Chair of the Theatre Trust. He is middle-aged and greying, a pompous bully who has long since lost sight of any ideals he may have had, if he ever had any. His only saving grace is his energy and initiative. He is domineering, bullying and aggressive in everything he does and says but he is a man with a purpose and has plenty of energy. His stance and persona should suggest this right away.

Other plays by Bettine Manktelow
published by Samuel French Ltd

Curtain Up on Murder
Death Walked In
They Call it Murder

ACT I

The General Manager's office at the Thurlow Playhouse. Morning. Early March

There are doors DR *and* DL. *The door* DR *leads into the rest of the theatre, the door* DL *into the secretary's office.* UL *there is a window, slightly open. The back wall is covered with old posters and black and white photographs of past productions and stars; the wall* R *has a notice-board and mirror on it*

To the L *of* C *is a desk, set sideways next to a filing cabinet which is against the* C *wall. There is a chair by the side of the cabinet and a desk chair behind the desk. Underneath the desk is a waste-paper basket; on it are a phone, in and out trays, a diary, a blotting pad, pens etc. There is a large pile of post on the desk; some letters, opened, are in a separate pile from the rest*

There is a table with flowers or plants on it UR, *and a chair against the wall. There is an easy chair* RC

When the play begins, the secretary, Valerie Marshall, is standing by the desk opening the post, disposing of the envelopes in the waste-paper basket by her side as she does so

The phone rings. Val lets it ring for a moment, then picks up the receiver with an irritated gesture

Val *(into the phone)* Yes? ... Yes, this is Thurlow Playhouse — only there's no-one on the switchboard this early. You've got through to the Manager's office. ... Oh, you want the Manager? Well, he isn't in yet. Theatres don't usually start functioning until ten o'clock, you know. ... *(She sighs)* Yes, all right, I'll take a message. ... *(She does not write anything down during the following, however)* What is the name? ... Titlady? Is that correct? *(She spells out the name)* T. ... I. ... T. ... Oh, not *tit*, but *tip* — *(She spells it out)* T — I — P. Yes, all right. I have it now. ... Jonathan Tiplady. Yes — I've written it down. ... Yes, I'll tell him. *(She hangs up the phone and continues opening the post, putting the opened letters into two piles)*

Alec Partridge enters breezily DR

Alec Good-morning!

Val Oh, it's you!

Alec That's right, it's me! Who are you expecting?

Val I wasn't expecting anyone so early. You *are* early, you know.

Alec Sorry about that! (*He slides into his chair behind the desk*)

Val What's wrong? Couldn't you sleep?

Alec No, my wife was snoring.

Val It puts everyone out when the Manager's early.

Alec I don't think anyone saw me come in!

Val I haven't half-opened the post. You can have what I've done.

Alec All right. It's perishing cold in here. (*He moves to the window* UL) Too much fresh air in the morning isn't good for anyone. Who left this window open? (*He shuts the window*)

Val The cleaners I expect. To get rid of the smoke.

Alec I don't smoke.

Val No, but they do!

Alec Any chance of a coffee, do you think?

Val Shouldn't think so. The snack bar isn't open yet.

Alec I thought the staff got here at half-past eight.

Val Yes, they do, but you can't expect them to start work right away. They have to get settled in.

Alec Settled in?

Val Have a natter and so on.

Alec Oh, I see.

Val (*peevishly*) People don't just come to work for money, you know.

Alec Don't they?

Val No — social intercourse is important too.

Alec *Social* intercourse?

Val That's what I said.

Alec Oh, that's a relief. I thought you meant the other kind! I couldn't manage that at this time in the morning.

Val I should think not! Pity you couldn't manage it at home; then you wouldn't have to come in so early. I'll have to have a word with your wife.

Alec Please don't! She wouldn't know what you were talking about! Anyway, I had to come in early today. Someone is coming from the Arts Council at eleven to discuss a grant for us. Don't you remember? It's in the diary. (*He opens the desk drawer and brings out a diary during the following*)

Val I haven't read the diary. I haven't had time.

Alec I understand, but it's really important that we impress him or her, whoever it is. I can't tell by the signature whether it's a him or a her. (*He produces a letter from between the pages of the diary and consults it*) A. Murdstone, it says. Could be Allan or Alison.

Val Or Arbuthnot.

Alec Yes, or Arbuthnot. Why don't they sign their full name like I do? Alec Partridge. Everyone knows who I am.

Val That's true!

Alec Anyway, whoever A. Murdstone is, we must treat him or her right. Everything depends on that grant. Of course we can't admit that. We had to say it was for an innovation — something new.

Val Something new in this place. That's a bit hard to prove.

Alec I know — that's why we must be cagey. (*He begins to look through the post Val has opened, but without very much interest*)

Val What on earth are you going to say?

Alec Ah — improvements and all that, a revolving stage, more seats, you know the sort of thing, so we can attract bigger shows, tours of prestigious musicals, prior to the West End, and so on.

Val You'll be lucky!

Alec It's worth a try!

Val Anyway, if you *say* you're going to make improvements then you'll have to make them!

Alec Of course we will — but we can always slide a bit of money sideways to keep us going, raise our standards.

Val Raise our standards? That shouldn't be too difficult in this place. If they came to see the show this week we wouldn't get a penny. (*She takes a leaflet from the post box and pins it on the notice-board on the wall* R. *During the following she tidies up the notice-board rearranging the notices*)

Alec Have you seen it?

Val Last night.

Alec I saw the first night … So it hasn't improved?

Val I should think it's got worse. Why do you book these shows?

Alec They're cheap!

Val You'd never think it was a professional production; none of them knew their lines, and they literally fell over the furniture. They were worse than the Thurlow Thespians.

Alec That's saying something.

Val Another thing: right in the middle of the second act the roof started leaking.

Alec Not again!

Val They were taking part in what was supposed to be a tender love scene — and rain drops were falling on their heads. (*She goes back to the desk*)

Alec They didn't burst into song, did they?

Val No, but the audience did! (*She opens a large envelope and takes out a contract*)

Alec I've reported the leaking roof to the Council time and time again.

Val (*looking at the contract*) What do they say?

Alec They say it's because of the rain!

Val (*falsely*) Ha! Ha! Oh, look at this! (*She holds up the contract*) Gloria Productions have sent back their contract — unsigned. I wonder why!

Alec Oh — what a bl ... bally nuisance. Here, give it to me. Why should they do such a thing? Do you think it was just an oversight?

Val How should I know? I'm only the secretary around here. (*She finishes what she is doing, leaving a neat pile of post for Alex, the envelopes in the waste-paper bin and a few letters for herself*)

Alec Get them on the phone, there's a dear, and sort them out for me.

Val That's *your* job.

Alec I know, darling. I don't mean sort them out entirely, I mean get them on the phone and put them through to me. You know what it's like — one-upmanship: "I don't want to speak to his *secretary*, I want to speak to *him*", and vice versa. It's just a question of who gives in first!

Val That's just plain silly. I haven't got time to hang on the phone just so that you can prove you're more important than he is. Anyway, there won't be anyone on the switchboard yet. Oh, that reminds me, someone rang up just now. Some funny name ... Tiplady, that's it — because I thought he said Tit but he said Tip. He rang up just before you came in and the call came straight through so I knew there was no-one on the switchboard.

Alec What did he want?

Val To speak to you.

Alec What about, dear?

Val I don't know, I didn't ask him.

Alec Oh, well, I daresay he'll ring back if it's important. (*He picks up the telephone receiver*) Now, do you think there's likely to be anyone there now?

Val (*glancing at her watch*) I shouldn't think so. She's probably having a cup of tea in the snack bar.

Alec She's lucky! (*He rattles the receiver, then puts it down*) When *do* people start work around here?

Val You ought to know — you're the boss.

Val exits through the door DL

Alec Extraordinary girl! Quite got the hump this morning. I wonder why. I can see I'll have to do everything for myself today. Now then ... (*He picks up the phone*) Direct dial ... (*He consults the contract for the phone number*) I shall just have to give in, I suppose ... (*He dials, singing a line from "There's No Business Like Show Business"*) Oh — good-morning, Gloria Productions? Could I speak to Roger Smallparts? ... Oh, he isn't in yet. ... Is his secretary there? ... You are his secretary. Oh, all right. Could you ask him to ring me when he comes in, please? ... Partridge — like the

bird ... (*With a false laugh*) Ha! Ha! That's right. Alec Partridge —
Thurlow Playhouse.... Yes, righto. Thanks. (*He glances through the post,
humming to himself. He puts a small pile of post in his pending tray and
the rest he puts in the waste-paper basket; having cleared his desk he sits
back with a sigh of satisfaction*)

There is a knock at the door, R, *and Lulu Lynchpin, the Stage Manager,
pops her head round the door. She is wearing a worried air*

Lulu Can I come in, guv'nor?
Alec Surely, surely, do come in. Did you notice: was the snack bar open when
you came through?
Lulu No — they were all gossiping in the kitchen.
Alec Oh well, never mind! Now then, what can I do for you so bright and
early?
Lulu You'll wish you hadn't asked.
Alec As bad as that, is it?
Lulu It certainly is.
Alec All right — fire away!
Lulu (*sitting opposite Alec in front of the desk*) You know I don't mind what
I do for the amateurs ——
Alec Of course.
Lulu I mean, I'm a professional stage manager, but that's neither here nor
there, they hire the theatre and I'll do my damnedest to give them a good
show.
Alec You always do ——
Lulu They're doing *Oklahoma* the week after next ——
Alec Don't remind me!
Lulu And that Madam Mason is driving me mad!
Alec She drives us all mad. It's so awkward with her husband being Chair
of the Trust. I mean *I* can't say a thing.
Lulu I know it's difficult but the way things are going, you won't have any
staff left if you don't do something.
Alec Wait — before you go on! I feel a headache coming on ... (*He moves
to the door* DL *and calls*) Val — Val, dear!
Lulu You'll need fortifying. Wait till you hear!
Alec Oh God! My head!

Val enters L

Val Did you call?
Alec Yes, dear, I did.
Val Well, I wish you wouldn't. It makes me feel like a skivvy or something.
It's insulting.

Alec Sorry, love, thoughtless of me!
Val Yes, it was. What do you want, anyway?
Alec Oh, Lord I can't remember … Yes I do, aspirin, that's it! Aspirin. I can feel a blinder coming on.
Val Well, I can't provide aspirin. I'm not a pharmacist.

Val exits L

Lulu Alec, I don't know how you put up with that woman.
Alec Oh, she's all right. Not everyone can work in the theatre.
Lulu Why not?
Alec Such temperamental people for one thing.
Lulu But she's the worst of the lot!
Alec I suppose so, but I'm used to her. Anyway, tell me more about *Oklahoma*. Let's get it over with.
Lulu The worst is yet to come!
Alec Go on!
Lulu We're over budget.
Alec How much?
Lulu Five hundred quid — and we haven't stopped spending yet.
Alec I can't believe it! Didn't you tell her — *la dame* Mason?
Lulu I told her — but she just shrugged her shoulders.
Alec The trouble is, the Trust will be after *me*, not *her*, and her wretched husband will just sit there as if it's nothing at all to do with *him*!
Lulu Don't get upset; there's worse yet!
Alec (*bravely*) I can take it!
Lulu She wants corn!
Alec Corn — I thought she had that in the script!
Lulu No, she wants real corn. You know, where the "corn is as high as a elephant's eye" — that bit.
Alec Real corn! Where do we get real corn in March?
Lulu She says it's a challenge!
Alec A challenge! Was she drunk or what?
Lulu No, she was actually sober for once. At least I think she was!
Alec Then she's gone mad — she's gone stark, staring mad!

Val enters with two aspirins

Val You're very lucky — I found some at the bottom of my handbag! They just need dusting.

Val hands Alec the pills

Alec Oh, you're an angel!

Val (*going over to Lulu, accusingly*) Who's brought this muck in on the carpet? This office was clean this morning.

Lulu Sorry, I'm sure, but some of us do a bit of dirty work backstage, we don't have time just to sit around in the office polishing our nails.

Val I never sit around polishing my nails!

Alec Oh, she didn't mean you, dear, she meant me! Any hope of a coffee yet?

Val How should I know?

Alec I'm gasping! Be an angel!

Val Oh, all right, I suppose I'll have to go and see. I haven't really got time ——

Val exits through the door R

Lulu That woman!

Alec It's her sex life, I think.

Lulu What about it?

Alec She hasn't got one! Now then, where were we? Oh yes, real corn ...

Lulu And horses.

Alec Horses?

Lulu She wants real horses — you know, for *The Surrey with the Fringe on Top*!

Alec Real horses! We're running a circus now. (*He gulps down the pills, chewing them energetically*)

Lulu (*rising and leaning across the desk to Alec*) The crew won't stand for it. What they say is: who's going to look after them? I mean, think of the manure!

Alec I'd rather not. Oh, God, it gets worse by the minute, it really does!

Lulu It will get even worse before it's better.

Alec What do you mean?

Lulu She's coming to see you — Madam Mason. I really balked at real horses, so she says she's coming to see you this morning.

Alec Not this morning! I've got someone coming from the Arts Council this morning. Oh, no, not this morning. I'll have to give her a ring, put her off. (*He picks up the telephone receiver and dials*)

Lulu That wouldn't put her off — the cow!

Alec What? She doesn't want real cows as well as real horses, does she?

Lulu No, I was referring to *her* — she's the old cow!

Alec I see what you mean. Oh, joy, there's someone on the switchboard. (*Into the phone*) Hallo ... Wendy, how are you? Not feeling too good? (*To Lulu*) She's not feeling too good.

Lulu She never is.

Alec (*into the phone*) Oh, I see, women's troubles! Well, well, it was nice of you to come in. ... Yes, dear, yes. ... How awful! (*He grimaces to Lulu*) ... Yes, dear, Lulu's here, would you rather tell her?

Lulu shakes her head energetically

Oh, she's just gone. Never mind. Now, what I wanted was Madam — I
mean Mrs Mason — on the phone. ... Yes, on the phone. ... What! She's
just walked in the stage door! Oh no! (*He rises, in a panic; to Lulu*) She's
just walked in the stage door. She'll be on her way up. Oh, God! (*Into the
phone*) ... No, it's all right, dear. It's not your fault. Thank you, you can go
back to sleep now! (*He hangs up*)
Lulu There you are, you see. I told you she would!
Alec Is the bar open? I think I'm in need of a pick-me-up!
Lulu Don't worry about the bar, I've got something backstage — present
from the last show.
Alec Oh, don't leave me alone with la Mason! I just can't take histrionics this
morning.
Lulu I promise I won't be a tick!

Lulu moves to the door R

Val enters R *with three cups of coffee*

Val (*accusingly*) I've brought you a cup of coffee.
Lulu Thanks. I won't be long.

Lulu exits R

Val (*putting the coffee cups on the desk*) That's just like her; I go to the bother
of getting her a cuppa and she walks out.
Alec She won't be long. Anyway, I appreciate it. You're an absolute angel!
How can I ever thank you!
Val I'll think of something.
Alec The extra cup will do for Mrs Mason if Lulu is too long.
Val Mrs Mason. Who said anything about her?
Alec She's on her way up, apparently.
Val Why?
Alec To see me — about the horses.
Val What horses?
Alec (*with studied patience*) Darling, this is getting like an Inquisition.
Madam Mason wants horses for *Oklahoma*. Real horses! Lulu is quite
upset! I mean to say — real horses!
Val Well — it would look a bit silly with pantomime horses.
Alec But we can't ... We haven't the room ... We haven't the budget ... We
just can't.
Val Then tell her.
Alec *Tell* her? *Tell* Madam Mason. Have you any more aspirin?

Val I don't think so. You shouldn't take too many. They're not good for you in large doses.

Alec I've only had two! For heaven's sake, Val, it isn't exactly an overdose.

Val You should face life as it is, not try to bolster yourself up with drugs. (*She leans over the desk*) Anyway. What have you done with the post? There was much more than this.

Alec Most of it is in the waste-paper basket.

Val That is a silly thing to do. You can't get rid of it like that. (*She retrieves the post from the basket*)

Alec No, I don't suppose I can — knowing our cleaners.

Val I'll look through it for you.

Alec Oh, you are a dear! You must be feeling better.

Val What do you mean? There was nothing wrong with me before.

Alec I thought you were just a little itsy bit touchy.

Val (*furiously*) No — I wasn't.

Alec Oh, sorry — only I know you have a bit of boyfriend trouble now and again.

Val That's just like a man. If a woman is a bit down they always think it's something to do with sex.

Alec Or PMT.

Val Or PMT. But it isn't. It isn't anything to do with anything like that.

Alec Then what is it?

Val You wouldn't understand. (*Dramatically*) Just life. Just coping with life.

Alec It is trying, coping with life, especially in the theatre.

Val (*reproachfully*) I hate you coming in early. It always puts me in a bad mood. Have you spoken to Gloria yet?

Alec No, he wasn't there, Roger whatever-his-name-is.

Val (*relenting*) I'll get them for you. (*She moves to the door* DL) I suppose I'll have to play the power game, refusing to put you through until his secretary puts him through.

Alec That will make my day. You see, you can be nice!

Val I am nice!

Alec Yes, well of course ...

Val (*tearfully*) You just don't understand.

Alec Ah—please don't cry. (*He moves over to her*) You can always talk over your troubles with Uncle Alec, you know.

Val You'll wish you hadn't said that! (*She wipes her eyes*) I might take you up on it!

Doreta Mason (Dori) enters. She carries her handbag, and a large rolled-up poster

Alec You're welcome ... Oh, Doreta — how lovely to see you! (*He relinquishes his hold on Val and moves across to Dori*)

Val (*muttering*) I'll see about that call.

Val exits L

Dori Hallo, Alec.

Alec and Dori embrace briefly, kissing the air either side of one another's heads

Alec So nice of you to call in. Anticipating the visit I have coffee ready for you. (*He moves back to his desk*)

Dori (*sitting in the armchair*) No, thank you. I hate the coffee here, it's full of chicory.

Alec I wondered what was wrong with it. (*He moves behind his desk*) Now then, Dori, do come in and sit down ... Oh, you have. That's right, make yourself comfortable. (*He sits*) Now then, what can I do for you, or is this a social visit? Very welcome, I'm sure.

Dori I would hardly make a social visit two weeks before a production, would I, Alec? Much as I like to see you.

Alec No, no, of course not; only too glad to see you too, Dori, any time. Is it anything special or just a general chit-chat about the show?

Dori It's this poster; have you noticed anything about it? (*She unfurls the poster*)

Alec Yes, what a pretty colour, such a nice shade of green. I suppose that was to suggest the prairie, was it? All fresh and green! What's wrong with it? It looks all right to me!

Dori I thought it was all right too, but Clarence noticed it right away—it leapt out at him, so to speak. I must say I was cross with myself for not spotting it.

Alec Let me see. (*He goes over to her to scrutinize the poster*) Right date, right time, right prices, right production, your name underneath in big letters — very big letters — quite right too! No, I can't see anything ...

Dori It's the logo. (*Dramatically*) They have omitted our logo — the logo of the Thurlow Thespians.

Alec Oh, lawks-a-mussy!

Dori What?

Alec I mean, how dreadful! Who printed it?

Dori I'm afraid it was your printers, Alec — the printers you recommended.

Alec I see.

Dori I'm afraid Clarence insists you sort it out for me. He says you should get on the phone to them right away and give them a bollocking.

Alec Yes — yes, right away. (*He moves back to the desk and reaches for the phone*)

The phone rings as Alec touches it. Alec looks startled, looking first at his hand and then at the phone. He picks the phone up gingerly

(*Into the phone*) Hallo? Who's there? ... Oh, it's Gloria — I thought you were the printers ... Oh, you're not the printers. (*To Dori*) Won't be a tick ——

Dori Don't mind me!

Alec (*into the phone*) Is that you, Roger? Roger Smallpiece, I mean Smallparts ... Oh, it is Smallpiece. I'm sorry about that. ... No, I'm not being personal. I meant I was sorry I got your name wrong. Oh dear, where were we? ... Yes, yes — about "Don't Look Now, Your Pants are Coming Down". ... Er, yes, your next show. You've sent back the contract unsigned. Just an oversight? ... Oh, not an oversight? Then what's wrong? ... But, my dear boy ... Oh, all right, you're not my dear boy, but you can't have a Sunday get-in unless we charge you double time. What about our staff? ... Yes, I know it's my problem. ... Tut, tut. ... Language. ... Please, there are ladies present! (*He holds the phone away from his ear and grimaces at Dori; mouthing*) Swearing. (*He brings the phone back to his ear; into it*) Oh, well, if you feel like that. ... Yes, yes, I know we do it for the amateurs, but that's different. ... Why? My dear boy, if you don't know I can't explain. ... Well, I just can't explain — at least not at present. (*He smiles nervously at Dori*) Just think about it, dear boy. ... Yes — and the same to you! (*He hangs up*) How rude! It used to be sophisticated to swear, now it's just plain common — commonplace.

Dori It does one good sometimes, the odd expletive! Clarence always feels better after a real blind!

Alec Oh, it's different for Clarence. He can get away with it. Now that chap on the phone — Smallparts, or Smallpieces, I can never remember the chap's wretched name — expects some sort of priority treatment because he brings two or three shows here a year and always trying to screw me down with the guarantee. You know how penny-pinching these impresarios are!

Dori Yes, I know, dear. You seem to forget I once trod the boards as a professional. I know what these people are like. Temperamental for the sake of it! It must be so difficult for you dealing with such awkward people all the time!

Alec (*looking at her askance*) Er — yes it is.

There is a tap at the door

Murphy, the Front of House Manager, appears. He is carrying a bottle of brandy

Murphy Excuse me, Alec ... Oh, sorry — just wanted a word. It can wait. *(He tries to hide the bottle behind his back)*

Dori *(with a welcoming smile)* Oh do come in, Murphy. How nice to see you!

Alec Yes, do come in, Murphy, take a seat. You look out of breath.

Murphy Not really — I was just bringing something up for you —— *(He nearly drops the bottle)*

Alec Ah — a prop. You were carrying a prop.

Murphy No, it's real — nearly dropped it. Phew! It's medicinal brandy.

Alec Ah, yes, the medicinal brandy!

Murphy Lulu sent it up!

Alec What a dear she is! I needed it for my heart.

Dori I didn't know there was anything wrong with your heart.

Alec Oh yes, there is — it aches!

Murphy I thought that was your ar ... *(He means to say "arse")* Oh yes, of course, your heart. The girl is right behind me with some coffee.

Alec Oh, but we have coffee ... Never mind, don't put her off. It never rains but it pours here. Oh, perhaps I shouldn't say that in view of the roof.

Dori What about the roof?

Alec It leaks — on the stage. Quite a to-do last night Val said. Raindrops were falling on their heads!

Murphy Deuced difficult, what?

Dori You must do something about it before *Oklahoma*.

Alec Yes — yes, we will.

Dori After all, it doesn't rain in *Oklahoma*.

Alec Not ever?

Dori Not when the show is on.

Murphy We could always put in an extra song. Have the principals burst into *Singin' in the Rain*.

Alec *(laughing)* Brilliant suggestion, Murphy! You could prance on the stage and do the number — umbrella and all. I could just see you.

Dori *(crossly)* I don't think you're taking this matter seriously.

Alec *(deadpan)* Oh, but we are.

Murphy Shall I stay? *(He moves over and helps himself to a cup of coffee, leaving the brandy on the desk)*

Alec Oh — please do.

Dori Yes, I should like your opinion. *(She goes back to the armchair and picks up the poster)*

Murphy What about?

Dori This! *(She stands and unfurls the poster for Murphy)*

Murphy Ah — the poster for *Oklahoma*. Yes, good, aren't they? Really good. You must be really pleased with them, Dori.

Dori No, I'm not.

Murphy Why's that? Such a lovely green colour; that's to suggest rolling prairies, is it? Quite impressive, I thought. People have said what a lovely poster; I've heard them.

Dori No logo!

Murphy What?

Alec No logo!

Murphy Good Lord!

Alec Yes, the printers left off the logo — you know, that little symbol that goes in the corner of all the Thurlow Thespians' productions.

Murphy You mean — the one that looks like a pregnant fish?

Alec That's right.

They both laugh, then quickly suppress the laughter and look very grave

Murphy How awful!

Rita enters carrying a tray with a pot of coffee and three cups on it

Rita puts the tray down, her back to Dori

Rita Here you are. It's nice and hot, just the way you like it, Mr Partridge.

Alec You are a dear! A blessed sweetie!

Rita Oh — but you've already got some!

Alec That doesn't matter. Leave it! I need plenty of sustenance this morning.

Rita I thought you was a bit harassed. I was down by the switchboard when you spoke to Wendy, when Mrs Mason came in. I said to Wendy, I bet he could do with a livener.

Alec How very perspicacious of you!

Rita What? Now, now, none of that. I'm not — what you said! (*She turns round and sees Dori; unperturbed*) Oh, hallo, Mrs Mason. There's a cup of coffee for you too.

Dori Thank you, but I don't like the chicory. (*She sits back in the armchair again*)

Rita Well we can't take it out. It's in the packet.

Dori I just don't like it. Neither does my husband.

Rita I'm sorry. I don't know what I can do about that.

Dori You could order something different, couldn't you?

Rita I don't do the ordering. Mr Murphy does.

Murphy I'll look into it.

Rita Personally, I never drink coffee. It keeps me awake.

Alec Not at work surely!

Rita Oh, you — that's not what I meant. You all right, then? Is there anything else you want?

Alec No, we're all right, dear.

Rita (*To Murphy*) You all right?
Murphy Not half!

Murphy stands behind Dori and gives a very pronounced wink to Rita. He then draws a pair of frilly knickers out of his pocket and waves them at Rita. She glares at him indignantly and tries to snatch them. He waves them in the air and puts them back in his pocket. She tosses her head, shakes her fist at Murphy and gives Alec a quick look

Rita goes off

Alec (*with a puzzled look from Dori to Murphy*) I'm getting on to the printers right now.
Dori You *were*.
Alec I was ... What happened?
Dori You were speaking to Gloria. (*To Murphy*) He was speaking to his girlfriend.
Alec No, not my girlfriend: Gloria Productions. You know, Murphy, Roger Smallparts — I mean Smallpieces, or whatever; I can never remember the chap's wretched name.
Murphy Yes, I know who you mean. A bit precious, isn't he?
Alec Only in the nicest possible way!

The phone rings. Alec jumps, then picks up the receiver

During the following Murphy hands Dori her coffee, then offers her a drop of brandy. Dori makes a show of declining and then agrees. Murphy laces her coffee and his own quite generously

Alec (*into the phone*) Yes, Alec Partridge. ... Who is it? Good Lord! It's the printers, but I was going to ring you. ... Oh — I did ring you! How strange, I don't remember. ... Oh, the switchboard rang you, and put you through. Well, why didn't you say so? What do you want? ... What do *I* want?

Dori glares at him

Oh yes, I remember now. The posters for *Oklahoma* ... Yes, they're beautiful, positively beautiful. ... No, no complaints — oh, well, just one small complaint. The logo. ... Yes, you left off the logo for the Thurlow Thespians. ... You know, that little symbol that goes in the corner of the posters. ... Yes, it does look a bit like a pregnant fish. (*He laughs and then suppresses the laugh*) Anyway, you left it off. Only Mrs Mason —you know, she's directing it ... That's right, *that* Mrs Mason. (*He smiles*

nervously at Dori) Councillor Mason's wife. He's Chairman of our Trust
— that's just the problem! (*He glances at Dori*) I mean, you can see the
problem. ... Yes, well, she's really cross about the posters. ... Oh, the
posters were proofed? ... Who by? ... Mrs Mason herself.

Dori bristles

(*To Dori*) He says you proofed them.
Dori I may have done. I can't remember.
Alec She can't remember.
Dori (*grandly*) I still want them corrected.
Alec (*into the phone*) She still wants them corrected. ... Oh, that might do.
   I'll ask her. (*To Dori*) He says he can print out the logo and we can stick
   it in the corner of each poster. That would do, wouldn't it? Save having a
   reprint.
Dori Oh, no, I don't think so.
Alec Otherwise there will have to be a reprint.
Dori Then there will have to be a reprint.
Alec Are you sure?
Dori Of course I'm sure.
Alec (*into the phone; with weary resignation*) No, she says that won't do.
   There will have to be a reprint — rush job. It goes on in two weeks. How
   much? ... How much? Oh, Gawd! Just a minute. (*To Dori*) It will be three
   hundred and fifty quid.
Dori That's all right.
Alec But we're already over budget.
Dori (*sweetly*) I'm sure it will be all right.
Alec (*into the phone*) She's sure it will be all right! ... Yes, yes, go ahead!
   (*He hangs up gloomily*)
Dori (*pleased*) I like things to be perfect.
Alec Don't we all?
Dori Oh, Murphy, that reminds me. I think you should take down all the old
   posters while we wait for the new ones.
Murphy Surely it would be better to leave them up while we wait for the new
   ones — otherwise the public will think the show has been cancelled.
Dori That's not what my husband says. He says it's an insult to have the
   posters up without our logo. That's what he says!
Alec (*miserably*) Ah, well, if that's what he says! You'd better see to that
   then, Murphy — but not right away. I'm expecting someone from the Arts
   Council today, Dori. I don't think we should disrupt the displays before
   then, do you?
Dori I leave it to your judgment, Alec. Far be it from me to interfere! (*To
   Murphy*) I must say, Murphy, this is very good brandy. I'm not supposed

to drink because of the tablets I'm on, but I don't suppose one or two will matter.

Murphy Of course not. (*He pours Dori some more brandy*) Are you not feeling well — I mean, on tablets?

Dori Tranquillizers — I always take them when I'm doing a show.

Alec You haven't any to spare, I suppose?

The phone rings. Alec jumps and gingerly picks up the receiver

(*Into the phone*) I'm not here. … What? … Oh, yes, Wendy, what is it? … Mr Murdstone. … Oh, it's *Ms* Murdstone — from the Arts Council. That's right. (*To Murphy*) It's a ms not a mister! (*Into the phone*) All right, put him … her through. (*To Murphy*) On the phone — that's good, perhaps they're not coming. (*Into the phone*) Not on the phone! Here in person! No! (*He stands up in panic and then sits down again*) But it's too early! … Where? … Right there! At the stage door! (*He stands up and then sits down again*) … Tell her to wait — no, no, I'll come down. (*He stands up again*) Say I'll meet her in the bar. … Yes, yes, the top bar. (*He hangs up*) I just hope they've cleared it up from last night, or at least emptied the ashtrays. She's here, the Arts Council lady.

Dori (*rising*) Good! I'd like to meet her.

Alec (*dismayed*) I really think, Dori, I'd better see her first. I don't know what she's like, what she's expecting ——

Dori What are you worried about, Alec? She's only human! What's the problem?

Alec So much rests on this grant, Dori. It's a matter of life and death!

Dori Whose life and death?

Alec Well — mine, mostly.

Dori Then I'll come with you — to bolster you up. You look as if you need bolstering up!

Alec (*in a panic*) No, no, I don't. The last thing I need is bolstering up! (*He gives Murphy a pleading look*) I mean, I think Murphy wants to have a word with you, Dori, and then, certainly then, I'll bring her up here. That's what I'll do; I'll order some more coffee and bring the lady up here to meet you.

Dori (*sitting again*) Oh, all right.

Murphy Yes — I do want to have a word with you, Dori.

Dori What about?

Murphy (*thinking*) Er … um …

Alec Righto! I'll be off then. I'll just be two shakes of a lamb's tail.

Dori Don't be long; we still have to talk about the horses!

Alec Oh, yes, the horses! Why did I have to mention animals!

Alec exits R

Dori So ... What's it about — this word you want to have with me?
Murphy About ... About — (*inspired*) the First Night Party. Yes, that's it, about the First Night Party. What to order; numbers and so on.
Dori Just as usual, all the cast plus one guest each.
Murphy And the hangers-on.
Dori (*severely*) Hangers-on?
Murphy I mean the Trustees and all that, and all the others who invite themselves along. I just want to know how much we should spend.
Dori Spend? It doesn't matter, does it? The Trust will pay.
Murphy But the details, you know. Is it to be cocktails and nibbles or beer and buns? Which? I do need to know.
Dori I really don't mind. What about a combination of both?
Murphy (*dubiously*) Well — I suppose that's possible.
Dori Of course it's possible. You're so good, Murphy, at organizing things. Now — how about another little drink?
Murphy By all means! (*He pours brandy into Dori's coffee cup*)
Dori I'm beginning to feel much better. I needed a hair of the dog today.
Murphy (*pulling up a chair and sitting next to Dori* US) Like that today, is it?
Dori Like that most days.
Murphy Ah well, we all have our props!
Dori You are so understanding, Murphy. I must admit I did enjoy that little tête-à-tête after the last show. I've hardly seen you since.
Murphy No, I seem to have avoid ... I mean we always seem to miss one another somehow.
Dori We were both a little bit tipsy ——
Murphy Yes, we were a bit.
Dori I was a little bit worried — afterwards.
Murphy Why?
Dori Well, I couldn't quite remember everything that happened ... You know how it is; you wake up the next morning and wonder what you've said or done. Hasn't that ever happened to you?
Murphy Frequently, I'm afraid.
Dori I just hoped you didn't take me seriously.
Murphy Me? I never take anything seriously.
Dori (*piqued*) I hoped you didn't take it too casually, either.
Murphy No ... No, I mean you're a very attractive lady but you're married ... And someone like Councillor Mason ... Anyone would be a fool to mess around ... I mean, it's just asking for trouble.
Dori (*sighing*) Yes, I'm afraid it is — it would be, I mean! Ah, well!
Murphy It's not that I wouldn't like to — don't think that.

Dori and Murphy gaze into one another's eyes thoughtfully

Val enters L

Val Where's Alec? I thought he was here.
Murphy (*sitting back quickly*) He's talking to the Arts Council lady in the
  bar.
Val Leaving you two on your own. How cosy!
Murphy You're welcome to join us.
Val I should just hate to spoil your fun. I'll take my coffee break now.

Val gives Murphy a hostile glare and exits DR

Dori What was all that about?
Murphy I haven't the faintest idea.
Dori Let's forget she came in. Where were we? (*She draws closer to
  Murphy*)

CURTAIN

SCENE 2

The same. Later

The CURTAIN *rises*

*Murphy is in the armchair with Dori on his knee. She is a little drunk and
becoming maudlin. Murphy is not drunk but is trying to keep Dori amused
so that she doesn't descend on Alec*

Dori So that was why I gave it up, you see, Murphy — I hadn't any backing
  from home and I was sick of being poor. My father always hated me doing
  it. Actresses, he said, are all tramps ... (*she hiccups*) You should get a
  proper job, he said, but by then I was, well — getting on a bit, and I'd
  already had one failed marriage, and then I met Clarence ... (*She sighs
  deeply*) But I always thought I could've got somewhere, given the chance;
  I always thought I could ... It isn't fair ... I could've been like — like ...
Murphy (*helpfully*) Joanna Lumley?
Dori Oh, no; dramatic — really a dramatic actress ...
Murphy Victoria Wood?
Dori (*rising and taking centre stage*) You're not making fun of me, are you?
  Eh, Murphy? You said you thought I was attractive? But now you're
  making fun of me? I should have met you in my heyday. I'd have made you

suffer! I used to be very attractive. I could've been a model, or something, if only I'd had the chance. You see, it all depends where you're born ——
Murphy Which side of the eiderdown?
Dori No — not that. I mean, take Marilyn Monroe.
Murphy I wish I could!
Dori She was born in Hollywood, so she was on the spot, so to speak, for anything that came along. Now if I'd been born in Hollywood — who knows?
Murphy Where were you born?
Dori Woolwich.
Murphy Yes, it is a bit different.
Dori Not exactly the West End. But that wouldn't have mattered if I'd had rich parents because they would've paid for me to live in Hampstead or somewhere and I would have been on the spot for parts. Agents ring you up and say "Are you available?" And you have to be available there and then. You know what I mean.
Murphy Yes, of course. I always thought you were available.
Dori Who knows what I might have been if only I'd had the chance!
Murphy None of us know that!
Dori I saw myself as Sarah Bernhardt — when she played *L'Aiglon*. (*She takes up a histrionic stance* C)
Murphy What?
Dori *L'Aiglon* — "The Eaglet". It was a play about Napoleon's son.
Murphy She played a male part?
Dori Oh yes — she was convincing enough to play male parts. That shows how great she was. I've always been interested in male parts myself.
Murphy (*intrigued*) Have you now?
Dori (*innocently*) They're so much better than female parts, actually. (*She moves back to him and sits on the arm of the armchair*) Did you know Sarah Bernhardt still had lovers when she was sixty-five?
Murphy Quite an achievement!
Dori I'd like to think I could do that — have a lover at sixty-five! It shows a spirit of rebellion, don't you think? Not only forking your fingers at convention but at age as well!
Murphy That's one way of looking at it. Still, you've got plenty of time left — haven't you?
Dori (*mischievously*) I'll tell you something. I haven't told anyone else. I haven't ever had a lover since I married Clarence.
Murphy (*embarrassed*) Oh well — do you want one?
Dori Yes. Frequently. I've looked, I've signalled, but nobody has taken me up on it.
Murphy They're all dead scared of Councillor Mason.
Dori (*wistfully*) Do you think that's it? It's not because I'm not attractive any more?

Murphy No, of course not. I told you that.

Dori It's so hard to know. Clarence never tells me I am, and I'm just not sure any more. Once upon a time I thought I was; men made passes; I had a lot of boyfriends, up until I married the first time — even afterwards, for a while.

Murphy And then you went and married Councillor Mason.

Dori I went and married Clarence. I still don't know why.

Murphy Nobody does.

Dori (*angrily*) What do you mean? Nobody does. Do people talk about us?

Murphy Oh, only in the nicest possible way. Why did such an attractive woman marry, well — Councillor Mason?

Dori Is that what people say?

Murphy Well — it is extraordinary. I mean, what did you see in him?

Dori I don't know. He sort of — took me over.

Murphy What do you mean?

Dori He made the decision for me. He was so forceful. I went along with it. It was so easy to agree. I was going through a bad patch. I was unhappy and on my own and awfully broke. Clarence offered me freedom, or so I thought. What actually happened is that I sacrificed the freedom I had to be myself to become — somebody else! Funny that, isn't it?

Murphy I suppose he could give you a good life style. Money — position ...

Dori I didn't care about that. Well, I suppose I did a bit. But mostly it was because he made me feel secure, and I don't mean just financially. There's a lot of security in not loving someone. You can't be hurt for one thing. I'd been there and I didn't like it. (*Suddenly aware that she is revealing too much*) Oh, I really am talking too much about myself. Why don't you stop me?

Murphy I think you should get it off your chest — whatever it is. It will do you good.

Dori Thank you, Murphy, You are kind! (*She becomes maudlin*) I've never told anyone else this before. But I'm not happy. I'm not happy at all. (*She cries*)

Murphy Don't cry! Your mascara will run.

Dori (*sniffing valiantly*) Yes, you're right. Thank you, Murphy. (*She instantly stops crying*) That reminds me: why do they call you Murphy?

Murphy That's my name!

Dori It's not your Christian name; I want to know your Christian name.

Murphy No, I never tell anyone my Christian name. That's why they call me Murphy.

Dori I wish you'd tell me ... We're friends now, aren't we? (*She slides on to his knee*)

Murphy Oh yes, getting drunk with someone in the middle of the morning is a sure way to make friends.

The phone rings. They both look startled. Murphy gets up, dropping Dori unceremoniously on the floor

Murphy Oh, sorry!

Murphy doesn't help Dori up but goes across to the phone and picks up the receiver. Dori gets up and sits in armchair

(*Into the phone*) Yes? ... Oh, Wendy — Alec is showing the Arts Council lady around the theatre. Who wants him? ... A man called what? ... Titlady? God, what with Smallpiece and Titlady I think someone is playing a joke! Do you know what it's about? ... No, Val isn't here either ... Just take a message, or ask him to ring back. Sorry I can't do more just now! (*He hangs up*)

Dori What was that about?

Murphy Some bloke with an odd name wanting Alec. Probably a creditor.

Dori (*rising*) Do you think we ought to find Alec? He has been gone a long time.

Murphy No — no, he'll find us if he wants us. That is ... Where were we? (*He sits in the chair US of the armchair where he was sitting at end of* ACT I SCENE 1)

Dori (*wistfully*) Do you really find me attractive, Murphy? I should like to know.

Murphy (*guardedly*) Very attractive ——

Dori (*kneeling on the seat of the chair and draping herself over him*) You know there's something about you I like.

Murphy (*moving back slightly*) Is there? I wonder what it is?

Dori You're so macho — I even said that to Clarence. That Front of House Manager is a real man, I said.

Murphy I'm flattered.

Dori After all, in the theatre, there are not many real men, are there?

Murphy You've noticed!

Dori Couldn't fail to — that was something that put me off the professional theatre. I mean, I like men!

Murphy You could've fooled me!

Dori I'm hedonistically heterosexual.

Murphy I'm surprised you could say that.

Dori Why? It's true!

Murphy I mean, it's such a mouthful for someone in their cups.

Dori (*moving away from him and rising, grandly*) How dare you! I am not in my cups! Not a bit of it! Not a little bit! Don't you believe me?

Murphy Well ——

Dori You don't believe me! Look. (*She tries to stand on one leg*) Look, the stork trial! (*She topples over and lands on the floor at Murphy's feet with her head in his lap*)

Rita enters carrying a tray with a coffee pot and four cups on it

Rita Oh — sorry, I did knock.
Murphy It's all right ... (*He rises quickly*)

Dori slumps forward

It's not what it seems.
Rita Don't worry me what it is. (*She puts the tray on the desk and moves the previous tray to the small table against the back wall*) Your business I'm sure. I've brought you some coffee. Looks as if you need it an' all.
Dori (*grandly*) Thank you ... (*She tries to rise and falls back again. She remains sitting on the floor during the following*)
Murphy Where's the guv'nor?
Rita Showing that lady round the theatre. Really giving her the treatment, he is. Who is she, anyway?
Murphy From the Arts Council.
Rita Oh, heck! Well, they're coming up here, so you'd better do something with her ladyship.
Murphy They can't come up here, she's plastered!
Rita Then get her out of sight.
Murphy That's easier said than done.
Rita Put her in the other office — where's Val?
Murphy Taking her coffee break.
Rita Well, I didn't see her. Last time I saw her she was crying in the Ladies. I was going to ask her what was wrong but I didn't think she'd tell me anyhow. (*She attempts to get Dori to her feet*) Here, come on, give us a 'and.
Murphy A foot might be better.

Rita and Murphy lift Dori between them and with great difficulty take her across the stage to the door L during the following

Rita 'Ow on earth did she get like this?
Murphy The usual way — drinking!
Rita You supplied the drink, I suppose — trying to get your evil way with her, was you?
Murphy Do me a favour!
Rita I know what men are like. You seem to forget — I've been through it all. Men! I tell you what, Murphy, a girl is better off without 'em!

They exit into the office L and return without Dori

She can sleep it off. She must have had a skinful to get like that.
Murphy She's on some pills. They don't mix.
Rita Why mix 'em then?
Murphy It was unintentional. Thanks for the help. Here, give us a kiss before you go back.
Rita No, I won't. (*She struggles with him and snatches her knickers out of his top pocket*) And I'll have my drawers back an' all. Pinching them like that, trying to make out we was up to something. What a insult!
Murphy They make a good pocket handkerchief, that's all!
Rita I know where you got them from — you villain! They're the ones I threw on the stage when that pop group was here.
Murphy You're lucky I picked 'em up. They might have used 'em to polish their — instruments.
Rita Oo — you!

Murphy kisses Rita — a quick smacker

There are voices off R; Alec and Ms Murdstone

The door opens. Alec is in the doorway

Alec My office. They promised us coffee, so we mustn't be late ... (*He looks aghast at the sight and raises his voice*) So we mustn't be late.

Murphy and Rita jump apart

Alec enters the room, followed by Ms Murdstone

Alec Ah ... My Front of House Manager, Mr Murphy — and I think you've met Rita; she runs the snack bar, and she's an usherette, barmaid, general factotum around here, just about everything. This is the lady from the Arts Council — Ms Murdstone.
Rita (*gushing*) Pleasetameetcha, I'm sure.
Ms Murdstone How do you do.
Murphy How do you do.
Alec Now we all know one another we'll have our coffee.
Rita And I'll get back to work. (*She tries to stuff her knickers discreetly down her dress*)

Ms Murdstone sees this and frowns in surprise

If there's anything I can do for anyone — just ring!

Rita picks up the tray of used coffee things and exits with a silly giggle

Alec Absolute gem, Rita is! Such a hostess, would do anything for anybody.

Ms Murdstone Mm — yes, that's what I thought.

Murphy Coffee, Ms …?

Ms Murdstone Murdstone. Yes, please. Black.

Murphy Ah, politically correct coffee — good!

Ms Murdstone I beg your pardon?

Alec Where is Doreta? I told Ms Murdstone we would be meeting her here. We were rather a long time. (*He sounds hopeful*) Has she gone home?

Ms Murdstone takes her coffee, wanders DS *to the wall* R *and looks in the mirror during the following discourse*

Murphy She might have done.

Alec Don't you know?

Murphy She might have gone ——

Alec Where?

Murphy On a bender!

Alec A bender?

Murphy For all I know! (*He points over his shoulder to the door behind him, and mimics passing out*)

Alec Good God!

Ms Murdstone (*coming back to the desk*) I wonder if I might see the receipts for the last production, Mr Partridge. Much as I would like to meet the director of the next show, I cannot stay all morning, and the receipts are really more important.

Alec Of course, of course. (*He rummages in his desk*) I have them here. The last production, you say? Not the present production?

Ms Murdstone No, I want a complete set of receipts; the final set, not half completed.

Alec The amateurs are doing *Oklahoma* ——

Ms Murdstone I'm not really interested in the amateurs …

Alec That's a relief!

Ms Murdstone Of course, as you know, it is our policy to support local organizations, to encourage arts in the community, but nevertheless we feel that Arts Council support should go towards professional arts organizations of one kind or another.

Alec Quite so! (*He gives up looking for the receipts in the desk and looks in the cabinet against the back wall*)

Ms Murdstone After all, if we keep the theatre going on a professional basis, there is always room for the amateurs to tag along. They benefit simply by the theatre being here.

Alec My sentiments exactly.

Ms Murdstone And they are after all only indulging in a hobby; there is really no reason why the Arts Council should support them any more than the local Pottery Club.

Alec I never thought of it like that! (*He produces a file of receipts and slaps it on the desk with relief*)

Ms Murdstone There you are, you see, there is always more than one way to look at a problem. Now then, are these the receipts from your last professional show?

Alec Yes, that's right.

Ms Murdstone May I sit down to peruse them?

Alec Oh, yes, please do — peruse them, as long as you like!

Murphy scurries to find a chair for Ms Murdstone. He brings one to the desk; Ms Murdstone sits and looks through the file

Alec sidles across to Murphy, R

Alec (*whispering*) What on earth were you talking about — about the Mason woman?

Murphy She's in there ... (*He points to Val's office*) She's plastered.

Alec Plastered?

Murphy Drunk!

Alec Drunk.

Murphy I do wish you'd stop repeating everything I say.

Alec I don't understand — how did it happen?

Murphy holds up the bottle of brandy and tips it upside down

Alec Oh, God — it can't be true!

Ms Murdstone Mr Partridge ——

Alec That's me!

Ms Murdstone These figures don't quite add up.

Alec Oh, let me look; a small oversight perhaps.

Ms Murdstone Small? Fifteen hundred pounds!

Alec (*taking the file in some alarm*) I'll sort it out, don't worry ... (*He looks at a receipt*) You mean this sum here — is that what you mean, this sum here?

Ms Murdstone What other sum could I mean?

Alec Ah — Murphy, can you help?

Murphy and Alec pore over the file

Look — here ...

Murphy Hospitality — that was part of it.

Ms Murdstone Hospitality?

Alec Oh yes, I remember; the Chairman of the Trust knew one of the cast —
George Spencer, he's been in loads of stuff on television — and anyway,
the Chairman thought he should give him a party at the end, so he did!

Ms Murdstone That's hardly a cost to be put against the production!

Alec It is if the Chairman says so.

Ms Murdstone Anyway — that couldn't have cost fifteen hundred pounds.
What about the rest of it?

Alec The rest of it?

Murphy The rest of it?

Ms Murdstone The rest of it.

Alec That would have been the guarantee.

Ms Murdstone You don't mean to say you still give guarantees?

Alec We have to, to professional shows — or they wouldn't come here at all.

Ms Murdstone A show like this — "Knickerless in Gaza". You'd be better
off without.

Alec But the public like it!

Ms Murdstone (*triumphantly*) In that case you shouldn't need any help from
us!

Alec and Murphy are crestfallen

*Dori staggers in L, the worst for wear, her hair all over the place,
supporting herself by the door posts*

Dori (*very grandly*) Goo'-evening, I am Doreta Mason! (*She falls flat on her
face*)

CURTAIN

ACT II

The same. A few hours later

Dori is sitting in the armchair, sipping coffee. Councillor Clarence Mason is sitting behind the desk in Alec's chair speaking into the phone. Murphy is hovering attentively US

Clarence (*into the phone*) No, I just told you I am not the General Manager of the Playhouse, I am the Chairman. As such I have complete authority over all expenditure. ... I couldn't care less about the cost. It's my wife's production of *Oklahoma* and it has to be perfect, understand? ... Yes, send the bill to the Trust — it will be paid! (*He slams the receiver down*) That told them! Querying everything we ask for! Of course they will be paid. Alec will see to that.

Dori (*lethargically, as if coming out of a coma*) Have you got the horses, then?

Clarence I have. Two lovely bays! That will be a sumptuous scene. I can imagine it. Quite a good idea of mine! Real horses, why not? (*He hums to himself, then sings a line from* "The Surrey with the Fringe on Top") Real horses and real corn! That was my idea too! (*He paces about; boastfully*) Thurlow will have seen nothing like this production, I can tell you! What do you think, Murphy?

Murphy Mm — yes. Should be effective all right.

Clarence Not much enthusiasm! You should be enthusiastic; that inspires the public. I'm always telling Alec that.

Murphy Well, I am enthusiastic, in my own way.

Clarence Your own way isn't good enough then, man! (*To Dori; sharply*) What about you, Dori? Pleased with what I do for you?

Dori (*muttering*) Of course. You know I am. As long as we're not expecting too much from everybody.

Clarence What do you mean — too much? It's their job! (*With a sneer*) You're feeling better now, I take it?

Dori (*pulling herself together*) Yes, I don't know what happened to me. I just woke up on the carpet with Alec bending over me and that lady making a fuss.

Murphy Anybody can faint — you've been overdoing things, Dori, I wouldn't wonder.

Clarence (*smugly*) Quite so!

Dori I only had a little drink, honestly darling, just because I wasn't feeling too good. It was nothing to do with that.

Clarence (*with a sneer*) Of course not. Never occurred to me for the moment that it was anything to do with drinking!

The phone rings. Clarence goes back to the desk and answers the phone

Clarence (*into the phone*) Yes. … No, he isn't here; who is it? … What? Never heard of him. Tell him to ring back. (*He hangs up abruptly*)

Murphy Who was that?

Clarence Oh, some agent with a funny name — Titlady, something like that. (*He sits down again at the desk*) It's not my job to deal with the day to day running of the place.

Murphy Someone like that rang before; Titlady or Tiplady. I forgot to tell Alec.

Dori I used to know someone with a name like that — Jonathan Tiplady, that was it. I knew him in Rep.

Clarence One of your boyfriends, no doubt.

Dori Not at all — he was gay.

Clarence Ah, that would have made him safe from you, then, wouldn't it? My wife was quite a lady in the old days, Murphy, did you know?

Murphy (*embarrassed*) Yes, I mean, no, I mean was she? Ah — well …

Clarence (*significantly*) Yes, quite a lady.

Dori Clarence — please!

Alec enters through the door DR. *He looks flustered*

Alec I think all's well that ends well! I hope so anyway. Oh, hallo, Clarence, didn't see you come in. (*He moves over to his desk and stands awkwardly by his chair, wondering where to sit*)

Clarence Humph! So what happened with this Arts Council person? I'm sorry I missed her. How did you get on?

Alec Oh, I was very nervous to begin with I must say ——

Clarence You usually are. That doesn't impress anyone. If you don't believe in yourself, nobody else will.

Alec Oh yes, quite so. But it isn't my style, assertiveness, Clarence, as you know.

Clarence (*sneering*) I do!

Alec It was touch and go I thought at first. Ms Murdstone — that was her name, she insisted on being called Ms, but I find it so hard to say, somehow … anyway, she wasn't very happy about the receipts from the last play — the hospitality and so on ——

Clarence Humph! Knows nothing about public relations by the sound of it!

Alec But when I explained the necessity — and I also promised we'd be more careful in future ——

Clarence What? You had no right to make promises on behalf of the Trust! You don't have to crawl round these people!

Alec She did seem quite reassured.

Clarence Why shouldn't she be? A theatre like this! It's not as if we're asking for the earth! What is it, a few thousand, fifty, sixty? Nothing to them, is it?

Alec I suppose they have to be careful!

Clarence Why?

Alec (*flummoxed*) I don't know exactly — but there were one or two things, unfortunate incidents ——

Clarence Like Dori passing out in front of her!

Dori I didn't exactly pass out ...

Murphy No, no, of course not.

Clarence (*sneering*) Of course not.

Alec (*going over to Dori; affably*) Of course not. Are you feeling better now, by the way?

Dori Much better, thank you. I don't know what came over me. I hope Ms Murdstone wasn't too put out ... It wasn't that, was it? Because of that? Because of me?

Alec Oh, it wasn't that but whatever it was, Ms Murdstone was very understanding. When I walked down to the car park with her she laid her hand on my arm and said "Mr Partridge, you are doing a good job under difficult circumstances!" Those were her exact words.

Murphy She knew what she was talking about!

Clarence Humph! Did she? What did she mean — difficult circumstances? What was she getting at? This job is a doddle, you know that, I know that, why doesn't she know that?

Alec I wouldn't exactly call it a doddle, Clarence, not exactly.

Clarence Well, I would. You people — you have it handed to you on a platter. Look at the subsidy: subsidy here, subsidy there! Dipping into the Council coffers! I let you do that! You should appreciate it.

Alec But we need it!

Clarence Publicity, that's what we need — publicity (*he bangs the desk*) and better productions.

Alec But Clarence — you were the one who said we didn't need a publicity officer.

Clarence No — we don't. We don't need to *pay* anyone. If the shows are good enough word gets around. We need better shows, that's all. I wish I'd seen this woman. I'd have told her. Anyway what was the outcome? Do we get the grant or not? That's all I want to know.

Alec She couldn't tell me there and then, but I am hopeful. She really softened towards the end, I thought. I'm really quite hopeful — considering ...

Clarence Considering what? What do you mean, man? Make sense.

Alec (*nervously*) She did mutter something about there being too much amateur involvement, that was the thing that worried her. You can see her point. We always seem to lose money on our amateur shows which seems ridiculous when the cast are not being paid. And after all, if the Arts Council want to support the professional theatre, putting money in here isn't going to help much, is it?

Clarence glowers at Alec

(*Lamely*) If you see what I mean.

Clarence No, I do not! (*He rises to take centre stage; at his most pompous*) This is Thurlow. The theatre belongs to us. Local money built this theatre, local money sustains this theatre; if local companies cannot be supported, then who can? I never heard anything so ridiculous!

Alec Ah yes, but the Arts Council is a national organization, Clarence, not a local one. (*He moves to sit at his desk*)

Clarence moves back to the desk and sits so that Alec is left standing

Clarence That is the sort of weak, shilly-shallying reply I expect from you, Alec. That's why you're still in the provinces instead of managing a West End theatre. Weak, shilly-shallying thinking! I wish I'd met this woman. Is she still here? I'll have a word with her. I'll sort her out.

Alec (*hopefully*) I think she's gone.

Clarence Find out! Ring the stage door.

Alec (*desperately*) I'm sure she's gone.

Clarence I'll find out! (*He picks up the phone; into it*) Who's there? ... Is there somebody there? (*He rattles the phone rest. Into the phone*) Here, girl — you should be on the ball; keeping me waiting. ... You know damned well who it is: Councillor Mason. ... Yes, that's better (*To Alec, smugly*) That made her sit up! (*Into the phone*) I want to know if that woman has left the theatre. ... What woman? The Arts Council woman of course. ... She's in the car park. (*To Alec*) She's in the car park.

Alec Oh dear!

Clarence (*into the phone*) Go out and tell her to come to the phone. ... What? ... Against the rules to leave the switchboard! Who do you think made the bloody rules? Do as you're told! No, wait a minute, I've changed my mind. I'll come down, just tell her to wait. (*He slams the phone down*) Sometimes, Alec, your staff leave a lot to be desired! Who does she think she is? Some little chit on the switchboard quoting the rule book at me. You'd better keep on eye on her.

Alec Yes ... I will, of course, but she isn't well today — the time of the month.

Clarence Do you think I want to know that? (*He comes round the desk*) I'll go down and have a word with that woman myself.

Alec I'm sure she didn't mean anything by it — just doing her job ——

Clarence I don't mean that woman — I mean the Arts Council woman. That's who I shall have a word with. Too much amateur involvement, is there? My God, our shows are a darned sight better than some of the professionals.

Alec Yes, but that's only because the professionals are so awful.

Clarence What?

Alec No, I didn't mean that the way it sounded. (*He looks despairingly at Murphy*)

Murphy (*coming to Alec's rescue*) No — what Alec meant was ——

Clarence I'm not interested in what Alec meant, or didn't mean. He books the shows. Whose fault is it if they're awful? Not mine.

Alec (*tentatively*) But you do set the budget, Clarence ...

Clarence Oh, fiddlesticks! You should shop around. There are good shows out there, it's just finding them, that's all! That's your job, not mine! Now, I'll go down and get that woman back. I'll soon sort her out. Order some tea for when we come back.

Alec (*weakly*) I believe she's a very busy lady.

Clarence What? Are you telling me they are all too busy in the snack bar to get some tea for the Chairman?

Alec No, no, of course not. I meant that Arts Council lady is a very busy lady; that's what I meant.

Clarence Humph! She's not the only one who's busy. I'm busy too! I'll make that clear to her. She doesn't know who she's dealing with. Amateurs, eh? I'll soon sort her out. (*He points to Murphy*) You get the tea! (*He points to Alec*) You — come with me!

Alec But, Clarence, I ... .

Clarence stalks out

Alec looks at Murphy, gives a resigned shrug and follows Clarence

Murphy (*moving to the desk*) I suppose that's the end of our grant. (*He picks up the phone and dials*)

Dori I wouldn't be surprised.

Murphy Eh? Oh, sorry, I was really talking to myself. I'd forgotten you were there. No, I didn't mean that the way it sounded. Oh, Lord! (*Into the phone*) Rita, love, can we have some tea in the office? ... I don't know — five or six, whatever, and some biscuits — it must be nearly lunchtime. ... Yes, love, as soon as you like. (*He hangs up*) I'm sorry, I didn't mean to be critical.

Dori You should, though. You should be critical.

Murphy What — of Councillor Mason?

Dori Yes, it's what he appreciates, someone standing up to him. Alec should stand up to him, really. My husband simply hates yes-men.

Murphy What about yes-women?

Dori You mean me?

Murphy I didn't say so.

Dori You did mean me. But it does require an awful lot of energy to oppose him. He browbeats people into submission. Anything to get his own way.

Murphy Browbeats?

Dori Browbeats.

Murphy As long as it's not beats!

Dori (*with an enigmatic smile*) Ah — well …

Murphy (*aghast*) You're not saying he beats you!

Dori (*evasively*) He's a bully. All bullies are cowards. I used to stand up to him in the beginning but he just wore me down. Now, I just submit. It's easier!

Murphy I'm sorry!

Dori Don't be sorry! I'm used to it. It's pointless talking about it. I don't know why I am. It must be a truth day.

Murphy *In vino veritas!* Are you feeling better now, by the way?

Dori Why does everyone keep saying that? I wasn't ill, was I? I just passed out.

Murphy You hit the carpet with quite a bang! I was really worried.

Dori I didn't feel a thing. If you must pass out, it's better to be drunk! I must say I was surprised to find Clarence here when I came to.

Murphy It's all right. We told him you'd had a bit of a turn. I hid the brandy bottle.

Dori Thank you, but he does know I drink. He drinks as well, only not as much.

Murphy I hope it wasn't my fault. I felt responsible in a way ——

Dori No, no it wasn't your fault at all. I told you: the pills I'm taking … Anyway. I do drink too much. I suppose everyone knows that.

Murphy Well, everyone likes a drink, only not all the time and to excess. It interferes so much with the rest of your life, that's what I think anyway.

Dori The rest of my life is so awful, I don't care if it is interfered with.

Murphy You can always change it.

Dori I'm not sure I can.

Murphy Of course you can. Take charge of your life. Take your life back.

Dori Ah, that's one thing I can't do — take my life back. It's too late.

Murphy It's never too late!

Lulu enters in a panic before Dori can reply

Lulu Where's Alec?
Murphy In the car park by now with the Chairman. Why?
Lulu I need him!

Lulu exits quickly

Murphy Oh God, why is it in this place we simply lurch from crisis to crisis?
I wonder what she's worried about?
Dori It doesn't matter, does it? Backstage isn't your province.
Murphy No — I suppose you're right there. You don't think I should go and
try to sort it out?
Dori I'd rather you stayed here and sorted me out.
Murphy All right. (*He moves the chair from against the* R *wall and draws
it up beside Dori*) Where did we get to?
Dori Was I very boring talking about myself — you know, before ... ?
Murphy (*valiantly*) Not at all!
Dori You're just being polite. I'll bet I was. I'm sorry. People do tend to be
boring when they drink, unless they all get drunk together and then nobody
notices. But it is so nice to talk about oneself to a sympathetic person.
Murphy Am I sympathetic?
Dori I think you were sympathetic. It's all a bit hazy, but it seems to me you
were, from what I can remember.
Murphy It was only this morning, you know.
Dori It seems like years ago — and yet I feel as if I've never really known
you until today.
Murphy I wonder why that is ...

They sit quite close together and look into one another's eyes

Val enters R

Val (*glaring at Murphy and Dori*) Oh, are you still here? (*She moves to the
door of her office*)
Murphy (*leaping up*) Val — dear.
Val Don't you dear me!

Val exits into her office

Dori Why is she upset? You're not ... ? I mean are you — an item?
Murphy Sort of.
Dori Sorry! I always thought it was the usherettes you chased after.
Murphy Oh, no, the usherettes are just a perk of the job. Val — she's a bit
special.

Dori You'd better go and make it up with her, then.
Murphy I'll try. Are you sure?
Dori Yes, definitely. I'm going home soon anyway. I think I can stand now!

Murphy moves his chair back to the R wall and then taps tentatively on the door L

Val (*off*) Come in ...

Murphy exits into Val's office

Val (*off; her voice raised*) What do you mean by it, you gigolo?
Murphy (*off; his voice raised*) It was nothing — don't be silly!

They continue to argue off-stage, their actual words indistinct, until the door closes

Dori, sighing, reaches for her handbag and takes out her mirror, looks at her face critically, then touches up her lipstick

There are voices off R

Alec, Clarence and Ms Murdstone enter, all looking grim. They are followed by Rita with a large tray containing a pot of tea, cups and saucers, milk and sugar etc.

Alec (*apologetically*) I'm awfully sorry to bring you back, Ms Murdstone, but Councillor Mason really felt ——
Clarence No apologies please—I know what I felt. Put that tray down there, girl, on that table.

Rita puts the tray on the table against the back wall. During the following, she pours out tea and takes it round to people, then exits R

Dori and Alec refuse tea

(*To Ms Murdstone, indicating the chair in front of the desk*) Take a seat. (*He walks behind the desk and sits in Alec's chair*)

During the following, Alec hovers in the background, wondering where to sit; eventually he settles for the chair DS of the R door

Now then — Ms Murdstone ...

Ms Murdstone I must say, Mr Mason, I do not appreciate being asked to come back like this. I have another call to make in precisely one hour and I have to get there. Furthermore I am used to dealing with the professional employees of whatever organization makes an application to us, not to the members of the board.

Clarence (*testily*) I am *Councillor* Mason, not Mr Mason, and I am not just a member of the board, I am Chairman of the board, Chairman of the Trustees! (*He rises threateningly*) As such I carry a great deal of influence.

Ms Murdstone But your influence is not the issue here, Councillor Mason. I think I should remind you that *you* are asking *us* for a grant, not the other way round. Your tone is rather unfortunate, to say the least.

Clarence (*blustering*) Unfortunate!

Dori (*rising*) I think I'll go.

Clarence No, stay — you might come in useful.

Ms Murdstone (*turning round*) Are you feeling better now?

Dori Perfectly, thank you! (*She sits down again*)

There are noises off L

The door DL opens. Murphy enters in a rush, followed by one of Val's shoes, aimed at his back. It misses

Clarence What on earth — !

Murphy Sorry to interrupt …

Murphy runs across the room and exits DR

Alec (*rising*) Oh, dear! I hope, Ms Murdstone, you'll ignore this … (*He moves to her, apologetically*)

Val appears at the door L, in a blazing temper and hobbling

Val Where did he go?

Alec (*pointing DR*) He went thataway ——

Val picks up her shoe. Holding it like a weapon, she exits R

Alec I hope, Ms Murdstone ——

Ms Murdstone Yes — I will ignore the interruption. Do you think there will be any more?

Alec No, I don't think so — we're fast running out of staff! (*He slinks back to the chair DR*)

Clarence (*attempting to be amiable but achieving the smile on the face of a tiger*) Ignore all that — this is theatreland. You can't expect it to be run like ... like the Civil Service. People here are temperamental. We're used to it. Now then — to business! Are we going to get this grant or not? We need to know; we must plan things.

Ms Murdstone It isn't entirely down to me ——

Clarence (*offensively*) Oh, don't give me that; I've dealt with your sort before. Don't hide behind that — "it depends what the Committee says" — I do that all the time when I don't want to give a straight answer. Your report will carry a great deal of weight, I know that. What are you going to say?

Ms Murdstone (*with prim determination, getting the original application from her briefcase as she speaks*) We have to be very careful, very circumspect with our grants. There are many deserving cases, needy cases. Thurlow Playhouse is only one of many. I would like to see some indication of thrift here. I should also like to see some input from another source ——

Clarence Cut the spiel. What do you mean by that? Input from another source. This theatre is heavily subsidized by Thurlow Council. I see to that.

Ms Murdstone Your amateur companies are heavily subsidized, Councillor Mason, more particularly — your own company it seems to me. What is it called — "The Thurlow Thespians"? Your shows always seem to run at a loss, Councillor Mason. I wonder if you can explain that.

Clarence (*rising, blustering*) I don't have to explain anything. I leave the accounting to the General Manager. It's up to him to keep an eye on the budget, not me!

Alec sighs deeply, his head in his hands

(*Strolling* DL) Anyway, the amateurs only make up about fifty percent of our input — we bring professional shows here on a regular basis.

Ms Murdstone Yes, professional shows, but of a rather low calibre if I may say so!

Clarence Not everyone wants Shakespeare.

Ms Murdstone I'm not suggesting that, Councillor, but there is a vast difference between Shakespeare and — what was that show called — "Knickerless in Gaza". You are not going to tell me that there is nothing in between the sublime and the ridiculous! I don't believe it!

Clarence (*moving back to the desk; furiously*) What I believe is that there are too many strings attached to this grant. (*He leans across the desk, wagging his finger in Ms Murdstone's face*) You can't imprison us like that — interfere in that way! Nobody can.

Ms Murdstone (*standing up to face Clarence; frostily*) I assure you I can. There are certain standards laid down ——

Clarence (*reverting to his normal character*) Don't you dictate to me, woman! I've run this theatre for twenty years. I was behind it being built in the first place. I've provided Thurlow with the best in dramatic entertainment ——

Ms Murdstone (*snapping her briefcase shut*) I quite understand your pride, please don't get me wrong, but in view of what you've said it does seem to me that you can get on very well without Arts Council support.

Clarence Of course we can't. We're in the red.

Ms Murdstone Precisely. You are in the red because of your own extravagance, Councillor Mason. That is all I have to say.

Clarence What do you mean — that's all you have to say!

Ms Murdstone That is all I have to say. I'm leaving now. Please don't come and call me back again. Thank you for your time. (*She turns her back on Clarence to address Alec*) Thank you, Mr Partridge.

Alec (*going over to Ms Murdstone*) Oh, thank you, Ms — er — shall I see you out?

Ms Murdstone Don't bother; I know the way by now. Good-bye. Good-bye Mrs Mason. I'm glad you're feeling better now.

Ms Murdstone sweeps out

Clarence Well — of all the sauce! Who does she think she is?

Alec (*grimly*) She knows who she is, all right! So that's that! Weeks of work for nothing, months of work almost — money too!

Clarence What do you mean — money?

Alec The elaborate accounts we had to cook up — I mean draw up ... They cost money, and they didn't fool her anyway.

Clarence (*smugly*) Can't be helped now. Who cares? We can't have these people dictating to us ——

Lulu enters DR

Lulu Guv'nor, I have to see you ——

Alec Well — you're seeing me!

Lulu (*glancing at Clarence, then back at Alec*) I need to speak to you ——

Clarence Go on — man, I mean woman, what's it about?

Lulu It's about *Oklahoma*.

Dori Yes?

Lulu The crew are refusing to handle horses. They say it's not their job. They're going to strike.

Clarence What? (*Rising*) I'll show them — where are they? I'll show them what's what.

Lulu There's a Union meeting backstage. Management are not invited.

Clarence Oh, no? Not invited, eh? I'll show them whether I'm invited or not. Just you watch me. (*He stalks across the stage*) I'll show them what's what! Strike indeed! In *my* theatre!

Clarence exits R

Alec Oh God, we'll really have a strike on our hands now. Do you want me, Lulu?
Lulu I'm not sure. I'm not sure if that will make it worse or better.

Lulu exits

Dori Oh, really — I don't care about the horses. Tell them we'll do without the horses. It wasn't my idea.
Alec It wasn't?
Dori No, it was *his* idea — my husband's.
Alec I thought it was yours ——
Dori No, I'd settle for no horses, no corn, simple sets, anything. It's him — he always makes my life hell unless I do exactly what he says, and most of the time it's only to get his own way. He's just being awkward. He can't help it. It's his nature.
Alec You shouldn't make excuses for him.
Dori I've heard you make enough excuses for him.
Alec Ah — but that's just to be circumspect. I need to keep my job.
Dori So do I!

Murphy enters R

Murphy There's a hell of a row backstage, Alec. I think you'd better go down.
Alec I was afraid of that. Oh dear! I wish it was Christmas! (*He goes off* R)

Murphy moves to follow Alec

Dori (*to Murphy*) How's your head?
Murphy (*looking sheepish, rubbing his head*) Yes, she did catch me the second time — quite a good aim.
Dori You must have done something dreadful to provoke her.
Murphy (*sheepishly*) Not really; she gets jealous.
Dori What about?
Murphy Everything … Everybody.
Dori And she hasn't any cause — of course?
Murphy Of course not.

Murphy and Dori exchange amused glances

Rita enters with champagne in an ice bucket and champagne glasses

Rita P'raps I should've knocked!

Murphy No — no, of course not. (*He moves away from Dori*) What have you got there?

Rita Champagne. (*She moves to the desk and puts the champagne down on it*) Councillor Mason told me to bring it up from the cellar. He said you had something to celebrate.

Dori When? When did he say that?

Rita Just now going down the stairs. He said he scented victory — don't know what he meant.

Murphy Scented victory! What is he going to do?

Dori (*to Murphy*) Perhaps you'd better go and find out.

Murphy (*to Dori*) What about you?

Dori Oh, no — I'm staying here! I've caused enough trouble today.

Murphy All right ... Wish me luck!

Murphy exits R

Rita I don't understand what's 'appening.

Dori Don't worry about it!

Rita (*referring to the champagne*) What shall I do with this?

Dori Bring it here.

Rita Eh?

Dori This is just the pick-me-up I need. Will you join me?

Rita Oh, I don't know about that. Do you think we dare? (*But she takes the champagne to Dori nonetheless*)

Dori Of course we do. Who's going to stop us? (*She picks up the champagne and sets to work to open it*)

CURTAIN

SCENE 2

The same. Later

The champagne bottle is open, standing in the ice bucket on the desk

Dori is still in the armchair. Rita has moved the chair from against the back wall R and is sitting on it. They are both holding half-empty champagne glasses

Rita So that's the way it was. My mum was proper old-fashioned and she

said "If you're pregnant, duck, you get married or out you go" — so I did!
Get married, I mean.

Dori You must have been very young.

Rita I was — and he was my first boyfriend. The thing is, it was so romantic
to begin with. I mean, when we went to the pictures he used to sit and look
at *me*, not the film. Know what I mean?

Dori That must have been very flattering.

Rita Yeah — it was, while it lasted. The trouble is once we was married he
didn't seem to want to look at me at all. In fact, sometimes I thought he
couldn't stand the bleedin' sight of me!

Dori So what happened? I mean, in the end?

Rita Oh, in the end I told 'im to sling his hook, that's what. I 'ad my little
'ouse — Council, but so what, it's mine as long as I live there — and I've
got it nice. The kids are as good as gold. Four of 'em. I 'ad four in five years.
He would never let me take the Pill. He said women should be well stuffed
and poorly shod — oh, I suppose I shouldn't say that in front of you.

Dori I think I get the drift. And you haven't regretted it — getting rid of him,
I mean?

Rita No, not me! Why should I? I'm poor but I'm 'appy. At least now I know
the money I earn goes in me own pocket and not into 'is!

Dori That must be nice, to have money of your own! It's so long since I
owned anything. (*She rises to make her point*) My husband refers to
everything as his; it is *his* house, *his* car, *his* bed ... You know what I mean.

Rita Yes, you're his, as well!

Dori Unfortunately!

Rita You want to stick up for yourself, Mrs Mason, that's what you want to
do.

Dori My name's Dori ——

Rita Seems funny calling you Dori.

Dori That's my name.

Rita All right, Dori — you want to stick up for yourself.

Dori That's easier said than done. (*She pours herself another drink from the
champagne bottle*)

Rita That's what I thought, but it turned out to be easier done than said.

Dori How?

Rita (*sliding into the armchair*) When I turfed my old man out I was the
'appiest woman alive; so were the kids. Tyrant, he was: "Do this! Do that!
Who's paying the bills?" — you know the sort of thing? Kept me short of
money while he spent all of his down the pub or in the betting shop,
knocked me about — if I said anything.

Dori (*leaning against the desk*) I just hate that sort of thing!

Rita I put up with it for a long while because of the kids, but the last straw
was when I found out he was knocking off some floozy down the road; right

little tart, she was! But I bided my time; I waited till the next time he came
'ome in a rotten temper and landed me one and I called the police, slapped
a Court Order on 'im right away and 'ad him chucked out. Best day's work
I ever did.

Dori Was it that easy?

Rita Course it was! All it requires is the guts to do it.

Dori I wish I could.

Rita What — kick him out? Councillor Mason?

Dori Does that shock you? Yes, I'd love to kick him out.

Rita It's a bit difficult if you haven't grounds.

Dori Oh, I've got grounds!

Rita You have.

Dori Basically — the same as you!

Rita Cor — I didn't take the Chairman for a gambling man!

Dori No — not gambling, but everything else. Mean and domineering,
flaunting his other women — and so on.

Rita I'd never 'ave thought it! (*She moves over to Dori*) Other women! I
mean — who'd fancy 'im? Oh, sorry!

Dori No, you're right, but he pays for it — massage parlours and so on. But
that doesn't worry me — honestly. It spares me a chore.

Rita I know what you mean.

Dori No, I could put up with that. I have put up with it. It's demoralizing but
I don't really care. I don't care about him, you see.

Rita I expect you was like me — it was all right in the beginning.

Dori No, I don't think it was ever all right. I married him for the wrong
reasons, entirely. I didn't love him, not at all. I'd been in love before and
got hurt, so I married Clarence for security, but that was stupid of me. In
the end the only thing that really matters is love. Don't you think so, Rita?
What do you think? I'd like to know, I really would.

Rita I suppose so, but love hasn't done me much good! Given me four kids
and worn me out, that's about all!

Dori There's time for it to happen again — you'll see.

Rita Do you reckon so?

Dori Never say die!

Rita What about you then? Cor, I never thought I'd be talkin' like this to the
Chairman's wife — I never did!

Dori Why ever not? I'm only human.

Rita Well — if you don't mind me saying so, Dori, some of us never thought
you was ... Not like other women anyway.

Dori (*hurt*) That was my husband's fault. That was the way he made me. He's
tried to mould me, make me more like him, and day by day I could see
myself becoming like him, and I hate it. (*She moves DL*) I'm like a lackey
— fawning on him for favours, out of habit, but at the back of my mind

despising myself for not standing up to him, just as I despise anyone who doesn't stand up to me.

Rita You should leave 'im. That would teach 'im a lesson. It's not as if you've got kids to consider ... Oh, sorry, I didn't mean that ——

Dori Don't worry, Rita. I'm glad I haven't got kids the way things have turned out. But as for leaving him? What would I live on? (*She slumps into the armchair, cradling her drink*)

Rita You'd be all right. You'd get a job, support yourself. I'm telling you it's great to be independent. I don't care 'ow poor I am, what I 'ave is me own! No bastard is going to come along and take it from me!

Dori That's great! The trouble is I don't own anything.

Rita You own 'alf of what he's got, that's your right. You can get 'alf his pension now, an' all.

Dori Half his pension ... He'd never let me!

Rita That's the law: he'd 'ave to, and you could make 'im. We women 'ave to look after ourselves, love. Why should men 'ave it all their own way? They 'ave for centuries. Now it's our turn!

Dori I wish it was mine.

Rita It can be. (*She sits on the arm of the chair*) What 'ave you got on 'im? There must be something apart from the massage parlour. 'As he ever hit you?

Dori Yes, quite often, but only in the most casual way, just when he was out of sorts or losing the argument. It was nothing personal.

Rita Well, I think that's bloody personal! 'Scuse my French!

Dori It hurts one's pride more than anything else, I think. But I suppose that's partly why he does it. It's to show me who's boss. I've always kept it a secret. I couldn't bear to think of anyone knowing that my husband had so little respect for me that he would lash out when he felt like it, as he might kick a dog, out of sheer bloody-mindedness, so cold and casual as if I didn't matter a damn! I've always been too ashamed to mention it to anyone, before. The archetypal battered-wife response, isn't it? *I* was the one to feel ashamed.

Rita 'S funny that, isn't it? I did too. I never told no-one, not even my mother, not for years. (*She moves to the desk and replenishes her drink*) She used to say to me "Why've you always got bruises on your face, Rita?" And I used to tell her I was always falling down. She thought I was a right little boozer, I can tell you! (*She pours herself some more champagne*)

Dori Clarence never hit me where it showed. He was too crafty for that. I suppose I should be grateful he never hit my face; he knows how vain I am.

Rita I never would've thought it, what you're telling me.

Dori I never would have thought I'd tell you, or anyone else. I never have before but today has been one of those days — a truth day.

Rita 'Aven't you never confided in no-one? One of your friends? (*She moves* *to Dori with the bottle*) You've got so many friends. (*She replenishes Dori's drink and her own*)

Dori No, Rita, I haven't any friends, just people I know.

Rita Cor — that's sad! (*She sits in the chair against the wall* DR)

Dori We have a social circle, that's true, but that was all part of the façade. We were "The Masons"; that was something to live up to, the façade my husband had created of a good partnership, a happy marriage, people of importance in the local community — and do you know what? It was all built on shifting sand.

Rita Well, I never!

Dori He has crushed me, quite deliberately. He's made me into a carbon copy of himself; no life of my own, no opinions of my own, no real personality — except when I'm drunk! That's me, that's all I am. A carbon copy of my husband! I'm not a real person. People think I'm a bitch, I know. Yes, Rita, they do. You admitted as much yourself. But I'm only what he has made me. I'm his creation — and I'm sick of it, sick of it! Sick of myself!

Rita Oh, Dori, you poor thing. You must stand up to him, that's what, you really must!

Dori (*hopelessly*) Yes, I really must. But I need some Dutch courage.

Rita tips the bottle up. It is empty

The voices of Clarence, Alec, Lulu and Murphy can be heard approaching, off

Rita They're coming back. I'd better get some more.

Rita scurries over to the door DR *and exits*

Clarence, Alec, Lulu and Murphy enter

Clarence (*sitting behind the desk in Alec's chair, looking very pleased with himself*) That's that, then. We'll get on to the Job Centre right away. (*He picks up the telephone receiver*)

Dori What's happened?

Murphy Tell her the worst ——

Alec He's sacked them!

Dori Sacked them! Sacked the stage crew?

Clarence Of course I have, the whole bloody lot! You don't think I'm having *them* tell *me* how to run the theatre ... What the hell do they know about it? Load of yobs! (*He rattles the receiver rest*) Is anyone there? ... Oh, you are there. ... Get the Job Centre, right this minute. (*He hangs up*) There's plenty of people out of work; we'll soon get a crew together. Good God, what do we need anyway! Anyone can do it!

Alec We can't do this, Clarence. We really can't. There's a show tonight. How are we going to manage? It can't be done.
Clarence I've done it, though, haven't I!

The phone rings. Clarence answers it

(*Into the phone*) Ah — who's that? ... The Job Centre. This is Thurlow Playhouse. We need some men. ... How many and what for? (*He looks at Lulu*) How many?
Lulu (*gloomily*) Two stage hands, an electrician, a sound mixer, a carpenter, a scenic artist, an assistant stage manager ——
Clarence That will do! (*Into the phone*) Seven altogether: one must be an electrician, one a carpenter, one a scenic artist, one a sound mixer, the others just yobs who can move scenery. ... Yes, wanted for Thurlow Playhouse. ... When? ... Right away, of course. ... I've just sacked the lot! ... What do you mean I can't do it! I've done it! ... All right, let them sue me. We'll pay. It's worth it. I'm not going to be crossed. So, what have you got on your books? ... Must they have stage experience? (*He looks at Lulu*)

Lulu nods vigorously

Well, I suppose it would help.

Alec groans and puts his head in his hands. Lulu and Murphy exchange despairing glances. Dori stares stonily out front

So what have you got? ... Nobody! Nobody with any theatrical experience? ... Oh well, never mind, send what you have got ... We'll teach 'em. (*He hangs up*) There you see, easy as falling off a log!

There is a pause

Lulu Alec, I'm sorry about this, but you can have my notice right here and now!
Alec Oh, no!
Lulu Oh, yes, I can't teach a new crew stagecraft in a couple of hours. It can't be done. I quit!
Alec But — Lulu — the show tonight. The show must go on.
Lulu Must it? Then *you* get the curtain up — you and the Chairman. He knows all about it. I quit!
Clarence You'll regret it! I promise you!
Lulu I doubt it!

Lulu exits R

Clarence Stupid woman! That's what comes of having a woman Stage Manager. I never did approve of it! We'll get a man. (*He moves to the door*) You can sort that out, Alec. I'm going home now. Coming, Dori? (*He pauses in the doorway and turns to look at her*)

Dori (*resolutely*) No.

Clarence (*moving back into the room*) What?

Dori I'm not coming home. I doubt whether I'll ever come home again.

Clarence What are you talking about? Have you been hitting the bottle again?

Dori Maybe I have a bit, but that doesn't matter. I know what I'm saying.

Clarence Take no notice of her, gentlemen, she's just having one of her turns — you know what women are like! (*Menacingly*) Come along, now, Dori — let's go home! (*He seizes her arm*)

Murphy I'd like to hear what she has to say, Councillor Mason, if you don't mind.

Clarence I do mind. Keep out of it!

Dori What are you going to do, Clarence? I can't imagine you'll hit me in front of witnesses. You never have. (*She gazes accusingly at Clarence*)

Clarence (*shocked; blustering*) Come on, Dori, don't be silly! Talking like that — hit you! I'd never hit you ... (*He wilts under her gaze*)

Dori (*rising and takes centre stage*) I have something to say.

Murphy We're listening.

Dori Clarence — you are ruining this theatre.

Clarence What? What are you talking about? I made this theatre. It was my efforts in the beginning ——

Dori Oh yes, in the beginning, twenty years ago. I'm talking about now. You've probably lost us the grant from the Arts Council ——

Clarence Of course I haven't!

Dori You have certainly lost us all our experienced stage crew and the stage manager. Your attitude ——

Clarence My attitude! You stupid bitch!

Murphy There's no need to talk to her like that.

Clarence You keep out of it!

Dori You put everyone's backs up. You always have. Your attitude ——

Clarence My attitude! This place is a joke. Run like a joke. The staff are all useless. "My attitude" — I like that. As for Ms Murdstone, I suppose you passing out under her nose just now had nothing to do with it? Or that little scene with Murphy being chased across the room, like some silly farce, with the secretary throwing things at him! My attitude! Humph!

Dori It was your attitude that was the final straw. That's what *I* think ——

Clarence (*moving to Dori; threateningly*) *You* think? What do you know about anything? A washed-up actress. You wouldn't amount to anything in this town if it weren't for me! What are you? Nothing!

Murphy (*moving* C) She's right about something — you are offensive!
Clarence What? Don't you start. You can be replaced very easily, my man, don't you forget it. Front of House Managers are two a penny!
Murphy If you want my resignation ——
Alec (*coming between Murphy and Clarence*) No, Murphy — stop now! Clarence — she's right.
Clarence What? What did you say? *I'm* right? I know that ——
Alec I said *she's* right — your wife.
Clarence Don't be such a blithering idiot! Who asked you, anyway?
Dori Clarence, why are you always so bloody rude to everybody?
Clarence Me — rude? Rubbish!

There is a knock on the door. Rita enters with more champagne; she stays in the doorway

Clarence (*shouting*) What do you want?
Rita (*nervously*) You asked me to bring up some champagne ——
Clarence Did I? When?
Rita (*stuttering*) I … I can't remember.
Clarence Neither can I! Take it back!

Rita looks startled, still standing in the doorway

Clarence (*shouting*) Did you hear me, girl? GET OUT!

Rita exits quickly

Dori There you see! You are bloody rude! And a bully. You only get away with it because you have a bit of power.
Clarence A *bit* of power?
Dori All right — a lot of power. You could close this place down at a whim, and you probably will do anyway, by bullying Alec into mismanaging it.
Clarence Alec doesn't need any bullying to mismanage anything.
Alec Thank you.
Clarence It's true! This place has been mismanaged from the start.
Dori Thanks to you!
Clarence What's got into you? You know very well I've been the backbone of this place from the beginning. They wouldn't have started without me, they couldn't go on without me!
Dori You started it, but you didn't know when to stop. You're the revolutionary who can't stop being revolting! You're killing this place, stifling it. Destroying what you created!
Clarence (*menacingly*) I think you'd better shut up, Dori.

Dori Why? Can't you bear to hear the truth? You're a megalomaniac. You
don't care about the theatre or the staff, you only care about yourself and
your little empire! You're nothing but a petty dictator. And if you can't
have your own way you'd rather destroy it all than see someone else take
your place.

Clarence I've had enough of this, Dori. You'd better shut up right now
or ——

Dori Or what, Clarence?

Clarence (*grabbing Dori's arm*) You wouldn't like to know.

Murphy *I* would though.

Clarence What?

Murphy I'd like to know. Are you threatening your wife?

Clarence Of course not. Just asking her to come home. (*Conciliatory*) Come
along, Dori, be a good girl. You know you don't mean it.

Dori Oh, but I do! And I'm not coming home, perhaps not ever.

Clarence Have you taken leave of your senses, woman?

Dori No, not at all — I've found them. I'm not coming home!

There is a pause. Clarence is at a loss, unable to cope with the situation

Clarence (*glowering at Dori*) Then what are you going to do?

Dori I'll tell you what I'm going to do. I'm going to stay here and help Alec
sort out the theatre, and first of all I'm going to suggest he quickly goes
down and begs Lulu and the crew to stay.

Alec Do you think they'll listen to me?

Dori Of course they will. If you tell them the Chairman has resigned.

Clarence What? You have to be joking! Me, resign — never! (*He turns his
back on Dori and looks at the others in disdain*)

Dori I think you will.

Clarence Never!

Dori You'll resign. Unless you want the whole town to know about your
weekly visits to the massage parlour in Lower Thurlow.

Clarence (*blustering*) Massage parlour!

Dori And how you beat your wife!

Clarence What?

Dori You heard me.

Clarence Don't take any notice of her, you two — she's gone mad!

Dori No, I've been mad, but now I'm sane. I've faced up to the truth today.
You are a bad man, and I'm sick of you. I'm leaving you.

Murphy Hooray!

Clarence (*turning on Murphy*) What has this to do with you? Is there
something going on here?

Dori There's nothing going on. You haven't got that excuse. In fact you haven't got any excuse. You either resign from this Trust, or I let everyone know the truth about our marriage, *everyone* — that means your colleagues on the Council, that means the poor hapless people who elected you, that means everyone who has had the misfortune to cross your path! They will all know that Councillor Mason is a bully, a womanizer and a wife-beater.

Clarence You can't prove it.

Dori I shall have a damn good try! Anyway, the mud will stick. It always does. You can't afford a dirty image in politics, you know that! You won't get elected next time. That's for sure!

Clarence (*dismayed, as Dori's words sink in*) Oh, Dori, but I'm up for mayor next year. Wouldn't you like to be my lady mayoress? Come on, say you would. All this is nonsense. Let's forget about it!

Dori I do not want to be your lady anything. I'm through! Don't you understand? Well and truly through! Kaput! Finito! Finished! I'm through!

Murphy (*applauding*) Bravo!

Clarence (*to Murphy*) I'm beginning to lose my temper with you.

Murphy (*moving to Clarence*) Oh, I do wish you would!

Alec Now then, we must remember where we are. We must behave like gentlemen.

Clarence You keep out of this, Alec!

Dori Gentlemen! (*She sits in Alec's chair. She has shot her bolt and is temporarily exhausted*) Don't ask the impossible from my husband.

Alec I really think, sensibly, we should all calm down …

Clarence I told you to shut up!

Alec (*with a sigh*) No, Clarence, I'm not going to shut up. This is my office, and I run this theatre. You seem to forget that.

Clarence Then run it — you nincompoop! You couldn't run a piss-up in a brewery, you!

Dori Don't start on Alec ——

Alec No, Dori, it's all right, I think I can defend myself. (*He confronts Clarence* DS) All right, Clarence, you want a showdown, fair enough. If your wife has the courage to stand up to you, so have I! This is my office, please leave.

Clarence What? How dare you!

Alec I do dare. You have put me in a very difficult situation. I shall have to call an emergency meeting of the Trust tonight and explain the situation.

Clarence Explain!

Alec Yes, explain that you have sacked the stage crew and virtually lost us the chance of Arts Council grant ——

Clarence That is clear rubbish! Anyway, the Trust will stand by me!

Alec Oh, I know you think you've got them in your pocket, but they're just as worried about bad publicity as you are. They want to be re-elected too! You might find yourself quite unpopular.

Clarence Don't try to blackmail me!

Alec I'm not. I just think it would be a good thing all round if you do as Dori suggests and resign.

Clarence (*moving to Dori, appealing to her*) Dori — this is your doing. You can't let this happen to me! Don't you realize what it means? I'll be a laughing stock in the Council Chamber! Losing the Chair of the Theatre. My enemies — you know I have enemies — they'll love it!

Dori I hope so! I hope it will all be worthwhile!

Clarence (*threatening Dori across the desk, his arm raised*) You bitch! You harridan!

Murphy I suggest you go now!

Clarence (*turning on Murphy*) I'll ruin you — you'll see. (*He points at Dori*) You ... You won't get a penny out of me! I'll chuck it away first, I'll squander it! You'll be penniless, in the gutter, like you were when I met you ——

Alec Your resignation, Clarence, right away if you don't mind. The future of the theatre is in your hands — or rather out of your hands.

Clarence Shut up — you puppet! Dori, one last time — if you don't come now, I won't let you in. I'll change the locks. I won't let you have any clothes ——

Dori Then I'll turn up with a reporter from the local paper, and a photographer. Would you like that?

Clarence Oh, hell! (*He looks round at all of them, a defeated man*) You'll regret this — the lot of you!

Clarence exits L

Alec, Dori and Murphy look at one another, then Alec gives a whoop of delight and skips across the stage. The three of them join hands and skip round in a ring. Alec begins sing "Ding Dong, The Witch is Dead" from "The Wizard of Oz". They join in, laughing

Val appears at the door R, looking even more mournful than before

Val What is going on? The Chairman nearly knocked me over on the stairs ——

Alec (*moving across to Val*) Val — darling — order some champagne! We are happy people! The Chairman has resigned!

Val (*pleased*) What! I can't believe it!

Alec It's true, it's true. Quick, get on to *The Mercury*, let them know, make it a story — then he can't change his mind. And ring up all the members of the Trust. We must have an emergency meeting tonight — seven o'clock.

Val looks astounded

Sorry, love, but it's urgent.

Val scurries across the stage towards her office

Wait, have you seen Lulu? Oh, I must see Lulu.
Val She's backstage with the crew. Everyone is. They're all talking about
what happened — him sacking the crew! They were going to walk out —
everyone, Front of House, bar staff, the lot, including me!
Alec Well, you don't have to now. Nobody will. I'll go and tell them. They
can stay. Oh, they will stay, won't they?
Dori Without my husband? Of course they'll stay.
Val What on earth made him resign?
Alec Nothing on earth! Something in heaven! Heavenly — a heavenly
messenger. (*He kisses Dori on the cheek*)
Val I can't understand what's going on here. Aloysius, can you explain?
Dori Who? Aloysius! (*She stares at Murphy*) No wonder you wanted to keep
it a secret!
Murphy Yes — you can tell why.
Dori (*amused*) But you told one special person. I understand that!
Val I wish I understood what was going on.
Murphy (*embarrassed*) I'll explain — later, I promise.
Val You certainly have some explaining to do.
Murphy But I can — you'll see.
Alec Please, darling, get on to *The Mercury* and I'll sort the champagne.

Val goes into her office, still looking puzzled

I'm so pleased! I'm so happy! I can't thank you enough, Dori! Fancy him
falling for that — how clever you are, inventing a story about an abusive
husband! Well, I never thought he'd fall for that.
Dori He wouldn't have done if it wasn't true.
Alec Good Lord! True!
Dori Of course. You don't think I'd make up something like that, do you?
Murphy You showed great courage.
Dori It was about time. Besides, you helped me.
Murphy How?
Dori Just by being here.
Alec Don't go away, you two, we've got things to do, but I must see Lulu.
First of all, Dori, we'll find you a job.

Alec takes Dori's arm and walks her DS

What about being our publicity officer? We haven't had one for years, thanks to Clarence freezing the post. Well, I'll unfreeze it, as from now. I'm taking back my power, and my first decision has been made. A job for you. Will you take it?

Dori (*throwing her arms round Alec*) Of course — delighted! You're a darling!

Alec (*extricating himself*) No, no, I'm not. You'll have to work hard but I know you will. Now I must see Lulu ... (*He sings a line from "Don't Bring Lulu"*) Oh, no, I mean, "do bring Lulu". (*He executes a little dance step over to the door* R, *opens the door, turns to Dori and Murphy and blows them a kiss*)

Alec exits

Murphy You've made him a happy man.

Dori He made himself a happy man. He stood up to Clarence at last!

Murphy No — it was you. You showed him the way. I admire you for it.

Dori I'm not sure I admire myself. Even if I have a job — I am now homeless!

Murphy I only have a small flat but ——

Dori Oh, no — don't even think about it! Men and I are finished for the time being.

Murphy I didn't mean ——

Dori No, it doesn't matter. Whatever you meant, it isn't a good idea. I'll be all right eventually. He's got to give me half whether he likes it or not. I'll manage. I'll think of something. You just go and sort out Miss Valerie. She looks as if she needs cheering up.

Murphy All right then. But I want you to know I do admire you. (*He kisses her on the cheek, respectfully*)

Dori Go on with you — Aloysius!

Murphy gives Dori a rueful look and exits L

Murphy (*to Val; off*) Look — can we be friends?

Dori sits behind the desk. She is looking very pleased with herself

Rita appears in the doorway with the champagne

Rita Am I right to bring it up this time? I don't want to get shouted at.

Dori You won't be shouted at, darling Rita, never again! At least not by my husband.

Rita 'Ow can you be sure?

Dori Because he's resigned, resigned as Chairman, and I'm leaving him! I'm taking my life back.

Rita Well, I never!

Dori It's true — and it's thanks to you. At least it's partly thanks to you! It's partly thanks to the champagne! But that's thanks to you too!

Rita (*giggling*) Oh, I can't believe it! Nobody has ever listened to me before.

Dori You said how easy it would be — and it was! So easy. I can't believe I've really done it. And I've got a job as well — Alec has asked me to do the publicity.

Rita Oh — that is good! I'm that pleased I can't tell you!

Dori Let's open the champagne!

Rita If you say so.

Dori I know how people feel when they overthrow a dictator! Long live the revolution! It's marvellous! The sense of freedom! *Freedom!* I'm *free!* (*Pause*) Homeless but free! That's a sobering thought!

Rita You don't 'ave to be 'omeless, love. There's a bed at my 'ouse if you want it, till you get on your feet. The kids can double up for a few weeks. You're welcome, love!

Dori Why ... That's nice of you, Rita. I might have to take you up on that.

Rita We girls 'ave to stick together, I say!

The phone rings. Dori answers it

Dori (*into the phone*) Hallo. ... Wendy? No, Mr Partridge is backstage sorting out the problems — except that the problems have gone away. Well, most of them have. ... Oh, I can't explain now, but we're going to be all right eventually. ... So what can I do for you? ... There's someone on the phone who's been trying to reach Alec all day.... I suppose Val could take it — (*She glances at the closed door of the office*) No, she's — otherwise occupied. Let me see if I can help. Put him through. (*She looks at Rita and covers the mouthpiece of the phone*) I'm about to start work.

Rita gives Dori a thumbs-up sign

(*Clearing her throat and putting on a formal voice; into the phone*) Oh — hallo, how may I help you? I'm the Publicity Officer, Doreta Mason. I'm afraid Mr Partridge isn't available at the moment. How may I help? ... You are? ... Jonathan Tiplady — oh, Jonathan! (*Her voice changes back to normal*) Do you remember me? I used to be Doreta Diamond. ... Yes, that's the one! Sharp and shiny! Well, I was then! ... Oh thank you, darling! You were quite a dish yourself! ... (*She winks at Rita. Throughout the following dialogue she nods and gestures to Rita, including her in the conversation*) Now then, what can I do for you? ... You've been trying to reach Mr Partridge all day? ... I'm sorry. We have had rather a busy time. But if there's anything I can do? ... Yes, I'm listening ... (*Her face lights up as she listens*) You're searching for a theatre to use as a film location! Your search is over, believe me! This theatre would be perfect. It's practically an antique! ... No, darling, not falling down, but loads of atmosphere and all a bit decadent — oh, you know what I mean. ... Who wants to do a mock-up when you can get the real thing? ... You're so right, Jonathan. So now then, what have you in mind? ... Of course I mean a fee. ... We're all professionals, darling. ... Five? Oh, Jonathan, do me a favour, not five — make it ten. (*She makes a thumbs-up sign to Rita*)

Rita claps her hands soundlessly

All right, if you insist, seven and a half! ... (*Almost shrieking*) What? Per day? (*She stands up and sits down again in consternation. Struggling to calm herself and sound casual*) Oh yes, I daresay that will do. Seven and a half per day! All right then. How many days? Ten? (*Faintly*) Did you say ten? (*She glances at Rita with incredulity*) ... Yes, yes, of course it will be all right. I promise you! ... It doesn't matter what we're doing. We'll find a way round it. Put the contract in the post. ... I'm looking forward to seeing you too, darling! Soon! (*She hangs up and stares at Rita*) Rita, I just can't believe it!

Rita What did he say? What's it all about?

Dori He wants to use the theatre for ten days filming at seven and a half grand a day!

Rita Thousands — I thought you were talking in hundreds!

Dori No, darling, film companies never talk in hundreds. Just think of it! (*She goes round the desk and hugs Rita*) We'll be rich! It will take us well out of the red and into the black. We won't need handouts from anybody! And I did it.

Rita On your first day!

Dori In my first hour! I can't believe it! Jonathan said he'd been trying to reach Alec all day. One more try and he would have gone elsewhere. What a good job I answered the phone! Perhaps I'm going to be lucky for the theatre after all.

Rita You've made a good start!

Dori Start the way you mean to go on, say I! Let's get Alec, Lulu, everybody — let's have a party! (*She picks up the receiver*) Wendy, dear, if you see the boss tell him to get up here right away. He will hear something to his advantage ... And Lulu, tell Lulu as well! (*She hangs up*) Just think if Jonathan had reached Alec this morning none of this would have happened.

Rita What do you mean?

Dori With that sort of money coming in we wouldn't need the Arts Council grant. Clarence wouldn't have got in a temper and offended Ms Murdstone or antagonized the crew, and I might never have had the courage to stand up to him. Think of that!

Rita I do hope you're not regretting it.

Dori Regretting it! Never! I'll tell you what, Rita, I feel as if I've been asleep for a hundred years and just woken up to a wonderful world!

Rita (*giggling*) The sleeping beauty!

Dori That's it! The sleeping beauty! But without the prince — and that suits me fine. (*She turns her attention once more to the champagne cork*) Now then, just knock on that door and see if they want to join us for champers.

Rita moves over to the door DL *but before she can knock on it the door opens*

Val rushes in in tears and runs across the room

Murphy enters close behind Val

During the following, Val and Murphy are oblivious of Dori and Rita, who watch with interest

Val (*as she runs, sobbing*) You beast — how could you?

Murphy Val, darling — I'm sorry ... (*He catches her* RC *and takes her in his arms*) I'm sorry — I'm sorry. It didn't mean a thing. Honestly, none of it meant a thing ...

Val Are you sure?

Murphy Of course I'm sure.

Val and Murphy embrace with passionate fervour, falling into the armchair

Rita Well, the old devil!

Dori Never mind, Rita — who cares? Just think what she's got to go through. You and me — we're free, we're free! (*She opens the champagne and pours a glass each for herself and Rita*)

Alec and Lulu enter R *and stand in the doorway looking at Dori and Rita bemusedly*

Dori and Rita raise their glasses

Dori To freedom!

Rita To freedom!

CURTAIN

FURNITURE AND PROPERTY LIST

ACT I

SCENE 1

On stage: Old posters and photographs
Notice-board
Mirror
Desk. *Under it*: waste-paper basket. *On it*: phone, in and out trays,
diary, blotting pad, pens etc.; large pile of post, smaller pile of
opened post, including large envelope containing contract. *In drawer*:
diary with letter between pages
Filing cabinet. *In it*: file of receipts
Two office chairs
Desk chair
Table. *On it*: flowers or plants
Armchair

Off stage: Two aspirins (**Val**)
Three cups of coffee (**Val**)
Large rolled-up poster (**Dori**)
Bottle of brandy (**Murphy**)
Tray with pot of coffee, three cups etc. on it (**Rita**)

Personal: **Val**: watch (worn throughout)
Dori: handbag containing mirror, lipstick
Murphy: frilly knickers in pocket

SCENE 2

Off stage: Tray with coffee pot and four cups on it (**Rita**)

ACT II

SCENE 1

Strike: Tray, coffee pot, coffee cups

Set: Cup of coffee for **Dori**

Off stage: Large tray with pot of tea, cups, saucers, milk, sugar etc. **(Rita)**
                Bottle of champagne in silver bucket with ice; champagne glasses
                (Rita)

SCENE 2

Re-set: Champagne bottle opened and standing in ice bucket on desk
                Chair for **Rita**

Off stage: Bottle of champagne   **(Rita)**

LIGHTING PLOT

Practical fittings required: nil
Interior. The same throughout

ACT I, Scene 1

To open: General interior lighting

No cues

ACT I, Scene 2

To open: General interior lighting

No cues

ACT II, Scene 1

To open: General interior lighting

No cues

ACT II, Scene 2

To open: General interior lighting

No cues

EFFECTS PLOT

ACT I

Lightning Source UK Ltd.
Milton Keynes UK
UKOW06f2348250516

275027UK00014B/228/P